VISITOR'S GUIDE
SEYCHELLES

Sue Heady

MPC

BIRD ISLAND (Île aux Vaches)

DENIS ISLAND (Île Denis)

The Inner Islands

0	10	20	30	40	50 km
0	5	10	15	20	25	30 miles

(H) Helipad   Airfield

Aride
Special Reserve

Curieuse Marine
National Park

Petite
Soeur

Curieuse

Grand Soeur

PRASLIN

Cousin Island Special Reserve

Cousin

FÉLICITÉ

Veuve
Réserve

Cousine

Marianne

Vallée de Mai
National Park

LA DIGUE

NORTH ISLAND

SILHOUETTE

Mamelles

Silhouette Island
Special Reserve

Sainte Anne
Marine National Park

Île aux Recifs

FRÉGATE

Morne Seychelloise
National Park

VICTORIA

St. Anne

Baie Ternay
Marine National Park

Cerf

Port Launay
Marine National Park

MAHÉ

INDIAN OCEAN

Providence

Picard Malabar

ALDABRA ATOLL

St. Pierre

PRI

GrandeTerre

Bancs Providence

Assumption

Menaï

Grande Île

FARQUHAR GROU

COSMOLEDO ATOLL

ALDABRA GROUP

Astove

Île du Nor

FARQUHAR ATOLL

Île

Goélettes

The Seychelles Group

0   50   100   150   200   250 km
0   50   100   150 miles

✈ Airfield

○ Bird Island
○ Denis

INNER ISLANDS
Aride
Praslin
Silhouette ○   La Digue
Frégate ○
MAHE

Area of Map at Left

○ African Banks

AMIRANTES GROUP
○ Rémire ✈
✈ D'Arros ○
Sand Cay ○   ○ St. Joseph's Atoll
○ Desroches
○ Poivre Atoll
Étoile ○

✈ Île Plate

Boudeuse ○
Deanoeufs ○   ○ Marie Louise ✈

INDIAN OCEAN

✈ Alphonse ○
ALPHONSE GROUP ○ Bijoutier
St. François

✈ Coétivy ○

LOCATION MAP

ERITREA
YEMEN
SUDAN   SOCOTRA   ARABIAN SEA   INDIA
LACCADIVE IS.
ETHIOPIA
UGANDA   SOMALIA   MALDIVE IS.   SRI LANKA
KENYA
TANZANIA
Area of Main Map
THE SEYCHELLES GROUP
CHAGOS IS.
INDIAN OCEAN
COMOROS
MOZAMBIQUE
MADAGASCAR
MAURITIUS
RÉUNION

Acknowledgements

I would like to thank everybody in both the Tourism Division of the Seychelles Government Department of Tourism and Transport and the Seychelles National Archives, but particularly Julien Durup, for all their help and information. Also Kanti for allowing me a free rein to rifle through his extensive 'library'; Ed Holloway, Speedy and the Fayons for ensuring that I had a roof over my head during my stay in Seychelles; and my father, Peter Heady, for reading and correcting my text. However I alone must remain responsible for any errors or omissions.

Published by:
Moorland Publishing Co Ltd,
Moor Farm Road West, Ashbourne,
Derbyshire DE6 1HD England

ISBN 0 86190 519 9

This book was designed and produced by
Camerapix Publishers International
P.O. Box 45048, Nairobi, Kenya

© Camerapix 1995

British Library Cataloguing in Publication Data:
A catalogue record for this book is available from the British Library.

Printed and bound in Hong Kong.

Photographs: Cover: Anse Takamaka on southern Mahé (photograph: Lindsey Porter).Page 1: Sailing boat at anchor off the coast of La Digue. Page 2: Takamaka beach on the south coast of Mahé. Title page: Fairy tern with chick. Contents page: Lily pond at the Plantation Club.

CONTENTS

Key to Symbols Used in Text Margin and on Maps

🚶 Recommended walks

☀ Garden/flora

✳ Other place of interest

🦆 Birdlife

🦌 Nature reserve/Animal interest

⛪ Church/temple

🏖 Beach/bay

🏛 Building of interest/ monument

Π Archaeological site

🏛 Museum/Art Gallery/crafts

⛰ Beautiful view/scenery, natural interest

🌳 Park/recreational area

✈ International airport

⛵ Fishing/cruises/watersports

How To Use This Guide

This MPC Visitor's Guide has been designed to be as easy to use as possible. Each chapter covers a region and gives all the background information to help you enjoy your visit. MPC's distinctive margin symbols and comprehensive index enable the reader to find the most interesting places to visit with ease.

At the end of each chapter an Additional Information section gives specific details such as addresses and opening times, making this guide a complete sightseeing companion.

At the back of the guide the Fact File, arranged in alphabetical order, gives practical information and useful tips to help you plan your holiday before you go and while you are there.

INTRODUCTION

Seychelles is an island nation of undisputed natural beauty. Its fantastic combination of granite islands, coral islands, atolls, marine life, fauna and flora makes a fascinating holiday destination, admired by all those fortunate enough to visit this tropical paradise. Be warned, however, that to visit Seychelles does have small drawbacks. Everything on the islands — from groceries to hotel rooms — is expensive because major foreign currencies do not buy many Seychelles Rupees at current exchange rates. This would be bearable if Seychelles lived up to its reputation as an up-market destination. But in fact visitors do not get good value for money. Although prices are high, hotels and their service do not equal the superb standards expected by today's international travellers.

Ancient history

Seychelles is unlike any other place on earth for one reason — the main group of inner islands are the only ones in the world made of granite. All other islands in the world's oceans are either coralline or volcanic.

The stark granite rock faces and, often precariously balanced boulders, strewn throughout the main group of islands are the results of huge movements of the earth's crust hundreds of millions of years ago. Then, the land mass known as Pangaea stretched between the two Poles and combined all of today's continents. Studies suggest that this single land mass was torn apart by continental drift, opening a space between Laurasia (modern North America and Europe — Asia) to the north and the southern continent, Gondwanaland. This space, the Tethys,

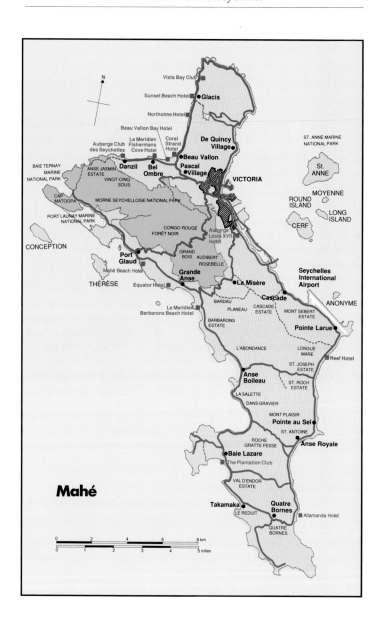

Mahé

N

Vista Bay Club
Sunset Beach Hotel • Glacis
Northolme Hotel

Beau Vallon Bay Hotel
Le Meridien   Coral   De Quincy
Fishermans Strand   Village
Cove Hotel   Hotel
Auberge Club
des Seychelles
• Beau Vallon
ANSE JASMIN • Danzil Bel   Pascal
ESTATE   Ombre Village •
BAIE TERNAY   VINGT-CINQ   VICTORIA
MARINE   SOUS
NATIONAL PARK
CAP
MATOOPA   MORNE SEYCHELLOISE NATIONAL PARK
PORT LAUNAY MARINE
NATIONAL PARK
CONGO ROUGE
FORÊT NOIR
CONCEPTION   Auberge
Louis XVII
Hotel
GRAND
BOIS   AUDIBERT
• Port   ROSEBELLE
Glaud
Mahé Beach Hotel GRANDE   • La Misère
THÉRÈSE   Anse
Equator Hotel   Cascade
BARDAU
Le Meridien   PLANEAU CASCADE
Barbarons Beach Hotel   ESTATE   MONT SEBERT
BARBARONS   ESTATE
ESTATE   • Pointe Larue

L'ABONDANCE   LONGUE
MARE
Reef Hotel
ST. JOSEPH
ESTATE
Anse
Boileau   ST. ROCH
ESTATE
LA SALETTE
DANS GRAVIER
MONT PLAISIR
• Pointe au Sel
ST. ANTOINE
ROCHE   • Anse Royale
GRATTE FESSE
• Baie Lazare
The Plantation Club
VAL D'ENDOR
ESTATE
Quatre
Takamaka   Bornes
LE REDUIT Allamanda Hotel
QUATRE
BORNES

ST. ANNE MARINE
NATIONAL PARK

St.
ANNE

MOYENNE
ROUND
ISLAND
LONG
ISLAND
CERF

Seychelles
International
Airport
ANONYME

0   2   4   6   8 km
0   1   2   3   4   5 miles

or Tethyan Ocean, included much of what is now the Indian Ocean. In time, Gondwanaland divided to create South America, Africa and Madagascar. India also broke away and was pushed north to join Asia, forcing the Himalaya mountain chain to rise in a process which continues, pushing the world's highest mountain range even higher. During the earlier part of this process the Tethyan Ocean was wiped out and, in its place, the Indian Ocean was born. In the midst of this great ocean lay an uninhabited group of islands — Seychelles.

It is not only that the granitic islands created from this massive movement of the earth's crust are unique, so too are the individual islands within the group. For example, on the main island of Mahé the dominant rock is an alkali granite, containing glass-like pieces of smoky quartz. On the second largest island, Praslin, the granite is often reddish grey in colour, due to the presence of coloured alkali feldspars. On other granitic islands, such as Curieuse and La Digue, wedges of coral well above the highwater mark indicate the story is more complicated. A fall in sea level as recently as 4,000 years ago, when ocean currents changed dramatically, led to this local phenomenon.

At one time, the islands covered a much larger land mass — all three major banks of modern Seychelles (the Saya de Malha Bank, Nazareth Bank and Seychelles Bank) were well above sea level during the last Ice Age when much of the planet's water was trapped in frozen waste. At that time, the land mass was perhaps 130,000 square kilometres (50,200 square miles) — nearly 300 times its present size.

Seychelles is composed of 115 islands, scattered across 1,340,000 square kilometres of sea. The total land mass of the islands covers only 455 square kilometres. The islands lie in the Western Indian Ocean, between four and eleven degrees south of the equator. They are 1,590 kilometres from the East African coast and 3,300 kilometres south-west of Bombay, India, earning Seychelles the advertising distinction of being 'unique by a thousand miles'.

The Inner Islands

The 115 islands of Seychelles are:

GRANITE ISLANDS

Mahé	St Anne
Praslin	Cerf (Île au Cerf)
La Digue	Long Island (Île Longue)

Round Island (Île Ronde)
Moyenne (Île Moyenne)
Île Cachée
Beacon (Île Sèche)
Anonyme Island (Île Anonyme)
Hodoul Island (Île Hodoul)
Rat Island (Île aux Rats)
Île Souris
Thérèse Island (Île Thérèse)
Conception Island (Île Conception)
L'Islette
Île Chauve Souris
Île aux Vaches
L'Ilot
Cousin
Cousine
Curieuse
Round Island (Île Ronde, Praslin)
Chauve Souris (Praslin)
St Pierre Islet (Praslin)
Booby
Aride
Zave
Félicité
Marianne
Grande Soeur
Petite Soeur
Île Cocos
Île La Fouche
Silhouette
North
Mamelles
Île aux Récifs
Frégate
L'Ilot Frégate

CORALLINE ISLANDS
Bird (Île aux Vaches)
Denis

OUTER ISLANDS
Plate Island (Île Plate)
Coétivy

AMIRANTES GROUP
Rémire (Eagle Island)
D'Arros
Desroches
Étoile
Boudeuse
Marie-Louise
Desnoeufs

AFRICAN BANKS
African Banks
South Island (Île du Sud)
St Joseph's Atoll, comprising:
    St Joseph
    Fouquet
    Ressource
    Petit Carcassaye
    Grand Carcassaye
    Benjamin
    Banc Ferrari
    Chien
    Pélican
    Vars
    Île Paul
    Banc de Sable
    Banc Cocos
Poivre Atoll, comprising:
    Poivre
    Florentin
    Île du Sud
Alphonse & St François Atolls,
comprising:
    Alphonse
    Bijoutier
    St François

FARQUHAR GROUP
Providence Atoll, comprising:
    Providence
    Banc Providence
    St Pierre
Farquhar Atoll, comprising:
    Île du Nord

Île du Sud
Manaha Nord
Manaha Milieu
Manaha Sud
Goëlettes
Lapin
Île du Milieu
Dépose
Banc de Sable

ALDABRA GROUP
Aldabra Atoll, comprising:
    Grand Terre
    Picard
    Polymnie
    Malabar
    Île aux Cèdres
    Île Michel
    Île Esprit
    Île Moustiques
    Ilot Parc

Ilot Emile
Ilot Yangue
Ilot Dubois
Ilot Magnan
Ilot Lanier
Cosmoledo Atoll, comprising:
    Menai
    Île du Nord
    Île Nord-Est
    Île du Trou
    Goëlettes
    Grand Polyte
    Petit Polyte
    Grand Île (Wizard Island)
    Pagode
    Île Sud-Ouest
    Île Moustiques
    Île Baleine
    Île Chauve Souris
    Astove
    Assumption

Some 30 rocks have also been given names by the Seychelles Government Survey Department.

History

No one can be sure who first set eyes on the islands of Seychelles, but it seems likely that it was Arab traders who began venturing south from their homeland after the advent of Islam in the 7th century. Arabic manuscripts from the 9th and 10th centuries refer to what are undoubtedly the Maldives (located in the northern Indian Ocean) and to the 'high islands beyond', which may be interpreted to mean the islands of Seychelles. There is also evidence to suggest that the 12th-century Arab navigators who mentioned the Zarin Islands were referring to what is modern-day Seychelles.

The first Europeans to make clear reference to the islands were the Portuguese. The navigator, Vasco da Gama, almost certainly discovered the islands in 1502 during the course of a voyage from Lisbon to India (to establish maritime trade links), given that in the same year he was made Admiral and the Amirantes (meaning islands of the Admiral) were named in his honour. A year later, a compatriot, João da Nova, named a group of islands (presently known as Farquhar) after himself.

And it was another Portuguese, Alberto Cantino, who drew the first map showing these mid-oceanic islands. From then on, Seychelles appears frequently on Portuguese maps as the 'Seven Sisters' or 'Seven Brothers' and 'Islas Mascarenhas'.

The first recorded landing on the main group of granitic islands took place in January 1609, when two ships of the British East India Company chanced upon the islands, thinking they were the Amirantes, while on their way to Aden and Surat to establish commercial links. John Jordain, a passenger aboard one of the ships, noted 'noe signe of any people that ever had bene there' and described the islands as 'an earthly Paradise'. The crew of the same ship recorded that they saw 'many coker nutts, both ripe and greene, of all sorts, and much fishe and fowle and tortells and manye scates with other fishe.' These written accounts support the theory that no one had settled the islands until this point in time. They remained largely uninhabited (except by pirates who may have used the islands as a temporary base) for another 150 years.

Given the enthusiastic accounts of John Jordain and the ship's crew, it is surprising that the British showed no desire to colonise the islands (or at least establish a staging post on one of the main islands). A possible explanation is that much larger prizes were to be won further afield

Cruiser cuts through the waters of St Anne Marine National Park

and that the coral reefs of the islands represented too great a hazard to navigation. However their natural isolation made Seychelles an ideal destination for the pirates who infested the Indian Ocean during the 17th and 18th centuries and perhaps used the islands for refuge and shelter. Prowling the Indian Ocean in search of ships to seize and bounty and riches to plunder, the unfrequented islands would have given them a chance to refit their vessels, reprovision and share out their booty far from prying, jealous eyes. Indeed, many relics related to pirates have been discovered in Seychelles and many islanders are convinced that fabulous treasures still lie hidden on Mahé, particularly in the vicinity of Bel Ombre. Piracy continued until well into the 18th century, when increased trade and shipping between India and Europe forced both British and French warships to hunt them down.

The Indian Ocean also became increasingly important in the middle of the 18th century, marked by rivalries between the French and the British for control of its expanses. In 1742, fears that the British were seeking a permanent base on uninhabited islands in the Indian Ocean — where they were likely to mount attacks on the French colonies of Île de France (Mauritius) and Bourbon (now Réunion) — prompted Mahé de Labourdonnais, then governor of the two islands, to send Captain Lazare Picault to explore the islands north of Mauritius and to try also to find a more direct route to India. Picault landed at Anse Boileau on the largest island which he named Mahé in honour of Labourdonnais. He then returned to Île de France laden with tortoises and coconuts. The islands looked promising for settlement and so Picault returned in May 1744 and anchored off what is now Victoria, on Mahé. A skilled mapmaker drew up accurate charts of several Seychelles islands and Picault reported that there was room for 300 plantations and the climate seemed suitable for all sorts of crops. Timber was excellent and the numbers of tortoise, turtle and fish prodigious. The expedition then returned to Île de France. It was at this time that the central islands of Seychelles acquired the names 'Îles Labourdonnais' and Three Brothers.

Before settlement could begin, however, war broke out between Britain and France as they both struggled to gain control of India. Twelve years elapsed before the islands were again visited by the French. In the meantime, the governorship of Île de France changed hands several times before Renee Magon came to power. Learning of the advantages of Îles Labourdonnais, he sent Captain Nicolas Corneille Morphey (born of an Irish father whose name was O'Murphy and a French mother, hence his allegiance) to take possession of the islands in the name of the King of France. This he did, landing on Mahé on 1 November 1756 and laying a 'possession stone', engraved with the arms of France to prove ownership. The islands may have been named in honour of a French Controller General of Finance, Jean Moreau de Sechelles. However, they may actually have been named after the influential French family of Herault de Sechelles, from whom Magon was seeking support and into whose family he later married. Seychelles had finally made its mark on the world map, although the spelling of the islands varied between Sechelles, Seychelles and Seichelles in Morphey's report. The only negative aspect that Morphey remarked on at the time, was the profusion of large crocodiles along the coast. These are now extinct.

The next step was to colonise the islands, but exploration was suspended once more, due to the Seven Years War (1756–1763) and the British-French Colonial War (1754–1763). Despite the 1763 Paris Treaty, which was a triumph for Britain, the French held on to Seychelles for another half century.

In 1770, Brayer du Barre, a French businessman, was given the exclusive right to settle on St Anne by Pierre Poivre, Chief Administrative Officer of the Île de France. The ship carrying the first permanent inhabitants arrived in Seychelles on 27 August 1770, with 15 Europeans, five Indians, and eight African slaves on board. Initially this settlement progressed well and du Barre asked Poivre for another land concession on Mahé. Poivre, keen to introduce spices to Seychelles to break the Dutch monopoly on the spice industry which was maintained through their outposts in the East Indies, agreed to establish a new settlement in the area now known as Mont Fleuri, just south of present Victoria. However, three months after the new immigrants arrived, in October 1771, the settlement was abandoned. At Anse Royale, another attempt to grow spices was set up in 1772. However, 'The Jardin du Roi' fared little better than its predecessor.

Six years later, when war once more broke out between France and Britain, France dispatched a garrison of soldiers to Seychelles, marking a formal period of French Government administration. The seat of power was based at 'l'Etablissement' (modern-day Victoria). In 1789, an administrator, Jean Baptiste de Malavois, arrived in the islands to develop agriculture and distribute land to new settlers. Encouraged by land concessions on Mahé and Praslin, as well as certain neighbouring islands, colonisation thus continued uninterrupted until the end of the century.

The year 1792, however, marked a turning point for Seychelles, for that was when Chevalier Jean-Baptiste Queau de Quinssi was appointed as French commandant of the colony. He guided Seychelles through the last years of its French administration, the uncertain years of the Napoleonic Wars — when it was unclear whether Britain or France had control — and, subsequently the early years of British administration. When Commander Henry Newcombe and his British ship *Orpheus*, accompanied by three other naval ships, sailed into Victoria in May 1794 he demanded the instant surrender of Mahé and its dependencies. As the head of a population of less than 2,000 Quinssi had no choice and handed the island, its dependencies, artillery and military stores, batteries and powder magazines to Great Britain, whose flag then flew over them. Quinssi, however, was left in authority. British interest in Seychelles was more concerned with ending the pillaging of their Indian Ocean fleet than with aspirations to create another colony. The British were content that they could sail into Victoria for fresh water and supplies, but that was all. So, as soon as the British fleet sailed out of sight, Quinssi lowered the British flag and raised the French, and life continued as before. In all, Quinssi is thought to have raised and lowered the flags around seven times, keeping everyone happy and maintaining peace.

By 1803, the population included 215 white settlers, 86 coloured settlers and 1,820 slaves. That same year war resumed between Britain and France. When Seychelles was declared neutral in 1804 the flags continued to fall and rise. Six years later, however, the British invaded and captured Île de France and Britain's sovereignty over all the southwest Indian Ocean islands was confirmed by the 1814 Paris Treaty. Although Britain had little interest in the islands, she needed to ensure France did not establish naval bases in the region which would challenge the security of their route to India. As a compromise, Réunion, whose port facilities Britain considered useless, was returned to France, while Île de France reverted to its old Dutch name of Mauritius. Seychelles was to remain a dependency of Mauritius until 1903.

Somewhat ironically, at the request of the British, Quinssi remained in office with the new title of First Civil Agent, Commandant and Judge. He anglicised his name to Quincy and died in Seychelles in 1827, when he was buried in the grounds of what is now State House. Because of Britain's general indifference, however, French language and culture still play a strong role in Seychelles. For example, Creole, the *lingua franca* is more a derivative of French than English. And Roman Catholicism remains the religion of the overwhelming majority of the people.

Seychelles experienced a dramatic increase in population in the early 19th century as people moved to the islands to produce cotton, which became the country's number one commodity thanks to an international reputation for fine quality. In the early 1820s, however, cheap cotton from America caused a slump in world prices of cotton. During the following two decades the slaughter of large whales — of which there was an abundance in the seas around Seychelles —

brought a new source of income to the islands.

The total population of free men in the country by 1827 was 685 compared with 6,638 slaves. When slavery was abolished in 1835, the vast majority were of African descent. The freed slaves, whose numbers were increased by the landing of other Africans taken from Arab slave traders by the British Navy, provided a labour force for the establishment of large coconut plantations (on which the economy would soon become dependent) and, late in the 19th century, the extraction of guano. At the end of the 19th century, export of copra began to improve the islands' economy and the population grew to almost 20,000. Slowly, but surely, the links with Mauritius were broken. Nine years after an administrator was appointed to preside over the executive and legislative councils in 1888, Seychelles was assigned a governor subordinate to the governor of Mauritius. But, it was only in 1903 that Seychelles became a separate British Crown Colony with its own Governor, the first of whom, Ernest Bickham Sweet-Escott, arranged to install a clock tower in Victoria (so named since 1841) and to introduce English into the school curriculum. The early 20th century saw a drop in coconut oil prices and Seychelles struggled to diversify into vanilla and other crops until the discovery of a synthetic substitute for vanilla

Tomb of Chevalier Jean-Baptiste Queau de Quincy, State House Gardens, Victoria, Mahé

undermined the fragile economy. These problems were compounded by World War I, which effectively cut Seychelles' trade links with German East Africa.

Despite being so far from the main battlefields of the two World Wars, Seychelles volunteers played an active part. The Seychelles Pioneer Corps joined the North African campaign which captured Tobruk from Rommel's Afrika Corps in World War II, and a number of Seychellois took part in the Battle of Britain as fighter pilots and airmen. The names of those who died, some 500 in both wars, are inscribed on the War Memorial in the Mont Fleuri Cemetery, Mahé.

During the first half of the 20th century Seychelles had little chance to develop, but after World War II, with the spread of modern communications and developments elsewhere in the British Empire, demands for political change began to affect Seychelles. The closure of the Suez canal made the route round South Africa's Cape of Good Hope more important for shipping, and Seychelles began to assume a strategic importance far in excess of its size. The first Legislative Council elections were held in 1948, although the vote was restricted to property owners. The following year the first district council was created and in 1963, the first political party. Rifned Jumeau founded the Seychelles Islanders United Party with the aim of improving living standards. But the beginning of modern Seychelles politics really began the following year when two young lawyers formed political parties. The Seychelles Democratic Party (SDP) was led by James Mancham while France Albert René headed the Seychelles People's United Party (SPUP). While the SDP favoured continued association with Britain on the grounds that Seychelles would not be able to survive on its own, the SPUP was strongly committed to achieving independence. However when universal suffrage was introduced in Seychelles in 1967, the vote went against independence.

As a result of the 1967 Suez crisis, Britain created the British Indian Ocean Territory (BIOT) which consisted of three Seychelles islands (Aldabra, Farquhar and Desroches) and the archipelago of Diego Garcia which became an American defence base by agreement with Britain. As part of the BIOT settlement Britain agreed to fund the construction of an airport for Seychelles. After the airport opened in 1971, tourism became increasingly important to the economy.

When Seychelles was granted a ministerial government, based on the British Westminster party political system in 1970, Mancham became Chief Minister. By 1974, however, Mancham felt that he had no option but to back Rene's call for independence and it was supported by most members of the Organization of African Unity (OAU). Seychelles became autonomous under the British flag in 1975 and the following year —

on 29 June — an independent republic. The two parties of President Mancham and Prime Minister René formed a coalition government and the three BIOT islands were returned to Seychelles.

On 5 June 1977, while the president was attending a Commonwealth summit meeting in London, a political coup d'état took place and the government was toppled. René, who became President, established a one-party state under which the people were represented by the Seychelles People's Progressive Front (SPPF). Naturally, there was discontent.

Three years later, in 1981, a group of mercenaries from South Africa led by Mike Hoare tried unsuccessfully to take control. Other plots were uncovered but in 1984 René was returned, unopposed, for a second five-year term as president. As a result of these political problems and lack of attention to tourism infrastructure, Seychelles' tourism industry suffered and the government attempted to diversify the economy, opening a tuna-canning factory and encouraging purse seiner fishing fleets.

René's third term as President, which began in 1989, did not reach a successful conclusion. The collapse of communism in Eastern Europe meant the loss of powerful support and the Commonwealth summit meeting in Zimbabwe in November 1991 made it clear to René that Seychelles was becoming more and more isolated. The onset of the Gulf War caused a drop in the number of visitors, causing the economy to falter.

In December 1991, President René announced a return to multi-party democracy. Mancham led the revived SDP, now more commonly called the Democratic Party (DP). When free elections were held to elect members of a consitutional commission in July 1992 the SPPF won 58.4 per cent of the vote, while the DP had 33.7 per cent. The opposition contended that the SPPF's control of the apparatus of State, including finance, gave it an unfair electoral advantage. The electoral commission proceeded to draw up a Constitution based on the demands of the SPPF. The opposition (DP and six minor parties) withdrew and united to oppose the resultant draft. Though it received a majority vote, the constitution failed to obtain the 60 per cent vote necessary for adoption.

An unprecedented alliance between Mancham and René followed. Each recognized that they could not continue alone amidst the call for national reconciliation. A new constitution based on compromise was drawn up and recommended by both DP and SPPF to the electorate. The minor opposition parties again opposed it, but it was accepted at a referendum in 1993.

The first multi-party general elections since the 1970s took place in July 1993. Eight parties contested the elections in which the President's SPPF won 58 per cent of the vote, 37.7 per cent of the vote went to the DP and 4.4 per cent to the young Parti Seselwa (Seychellois Party).

Despite the severe limitations of an island economy, Seychelles has achieved a Gross Domestic Product (GDP) per capita of over US$5,000, placing the country among middle income nations.

Food, Drink and Entertainment

Lovers of seafood will find their seventh heaven in Seychelles, where the staple diet is fish and local chefs have long perfected the art of cooking the abundant fruits of the seas that surround the islands. Far from serving up the same fish dish every night, Seychellois cooks draw on the menus of the three main areas of the world — Europe, Africa and Asia — whence their forebears came, to produce a full array of dishes.

Coconut milk is used in some island dishes, as are curry powders made according to ancient family recipes. Lime, ginger, cloves, cardamom seeds, cinnamon, garlic and a fiery chilli sauce — to the Seychellois what tomato ketchup is to many Westerners — are all frequently used.

Among local appetisers is *tec tec* soup, made from very small clam-like shellfish found on the beach. Islanders often dig for *tec tecs*, which burrow down into the sand once a wave has come in and receded, on beaches such as Beau Vallon and Grand Anse. Fish soup, usually made from the head of a large 'bourzwa' (red snapper), plenty of purple onions, tomatoes and, perhaps, sour 'bilimbis' which resemble miniature cucumbers, is common. 'Palourdes farcies' (small stuffed mussels), aubergine or octopus fritters make interesting alternatives to soup at the beginning of a meal, as does octopus salad, which is soft and succulent, rather than rubbery and chewy. Every Seychellois swears by his or her own method of making octopus tender. Some boil it with a slice of papaya and an old wine cork, others use a pressure cooker.

As a main meal, curries are popular with islanders. Fish curries, made of either tuna or bonito, are common and likely to be spicy and delicious. Octopus curry, on the other hand, is usually cooked in coconut milk and seasoned with sugar, vanilla and nutmeg, making it sweeter and cooler.

Variations of the fish theme include 'Kat Kat de Bananas au Poisson', a very popular dish among the locals, which is made with fish and green plantain (a type of cooking banana) cooked in coconut milk. Otherwise, fish is grilled Creole style, whole, topped with chopped tomatoes, onions, garlic, ginger and fresh herbs; cut into steaks, marinated and barbecued; smoked and eaten cold with a salad; or fried in batter and eaten with chips — especially for those from the United Kingdom feeling a little homesick.

Imported rice is another staple high on the list of local ingredients. However, the Seychellois are very fond of what are known as 'gros manger' — the root and tuberous vegetables of cassava and sweet potato, plus plantains and breadfruit when they are available. Breadfruit is so versatile it may be boiled, mashed, fried to make chips or baked on a barbecue. Breadfruit should be tried, if only because local legend says that those who eat the breadfruit will return to the islands.

'Chatinis', or chutneys, are an essential side dish to a Seychellois curry and are usually made from either freshly grated green mangoes, golden apples or green papaya lightly sautéd with onion in oil, finished with a fresh squeeze of lime. 'Chatini de requin', or shark chutney, is the flesh of a shark mixed with garlic, ginger and onion to make a delicious dish similar to a salad. Seychelles salads are normally made with a combination of sliced or grated cabbage, tomatoes, green peppers, cucumbers, onions and carrots with a light, refreshing dressing of squeezed lime or lemon juice, oil, salt and pepper. 'Patole', a long cucumber-shaped vegetable, and 'bilimbi', chopped or grated, are also popular in salads.

One unusual salad, known as 'Millionaire's Salad', takes its name from the fact that, originally, the very heart of the Palmis palm, an endemic species, was used to make the salad — and the whole tree had to be killed to obtain the centre of the palm. Now, however, it is usual to serve the heart of the coconut palm, together with lime and oil.

Speciality dishes tend to be extremely exotic in Seychelles. For example, a favourite food among the locals is fruit bat, either curried or as a ragout cooked in red wine sauce. The taste is similar to chicken, but the meat is generally much tougher than poultry. There is certainly no need to feel squeamish about eating fruit bat, for this animal lives a very clean lifestyle, consuming only fresh fruit — as its name implies. Seychellois also eagerly await the season when millions of terns return to their favourite nesting grounds on various outlying islands roughly between May and October. It is then that they harvest the small, spotted terns' eggs. Demand always exceeds supply, particularly as, in recent years, the number of terns visiting the islands has declined, perhaps not surprisingly. Although they do have a special flavour all their own these small seabird eggs are not at all fishy. The eggs are either boiled, fried, scrambled or cooked in omelettes.

If some of the Seychellois culinary delights sound a little too exotic, have no fear. All the major hotels serve international cuisine and there are French, Italian, Japanese and Chinese speciality restaurants dotted

Dancers perform the **moutya** *around a bonfire on Round Island*

Mouthwatering display of local shellfish

around Mahé.

Seychellois desserts are generally heavy, sticky and sweet — such as coconut ice, banana cake, caramel banana and pumpkin fritters. One speciality is a 'ladob', which is made with cooking bananas simmered in coconut milk with sugar and a vanilla pod. This turns into an extremely rich, tasty and satisfying pudding.

Lighter alternatives may be found in local fruit — several different varieties of seasonal mango, papaya or pawpaw, jamalacs (a conical-shaped white, pink or red fruit which is refreshing though not particularly flavoursome), oranges, passion fruit, guava and the ubiquitous banana. There are more than 20 varieties of banana in Seychelles. Two of the more tasty when eaten raw are 'banan mil' (honey banana) and 'banan figue' (fig banana). Various ice creams and sorbets are made on the islands — the one with the most local flavour is coconut — while the 'best choc ices in the world' (according to one trusted source) are made by Dominion Traders in Victoria's Market Street.

As for beverages, Seychelles produces its own bottled water, soft drinks, beer — Seybrew, Eku and Guinness — and a tropical liqueur called, 'Coco d'Amour'. Don't expect lots of exotic fruit juices, however. Fresh lime, with a little salt or sugar, perhaps, but other fresh fruit juices are few and far between. After dinner refreshments include a locally grown brand of tea, often flavoured with vanilla, and a refreshing tisane known as 'citronnel' which is made by pouring boiling water over wild lemon grass. For a truly Seychellois drink, try 'toddy', which is tapped from the top shoot of a palm tree, the dripping sap usually caught in a bamboo container at the rate of up to eight litres a day. Innocuous when first collected, it rapidly ferments into a potent brew — one strictly for the adventurous, as is 'baka', a crude form of alcohol made from juice expressed from sugar cane.

Night life in Seychelles tends to focus on the hotels — particularly during the week — as the Seychellois, early risers, tend to go to bed around 10 pm. Hotels often stage evenings of local entertainment when bands and *sega* troupes perform traditional songs and dances. In addition, the Mahé Beach Hotel has its own nightclub and there are casinos in both the Beau Vallon Bay Hotel and The Plantation Club Hotel. Apart from the hotels, several discotheques are popular with the locals, especially at weekends. Top of the 'in' places to be seen are The Love Nut and Flamboyant in Victoria and Katiolo's at Anse Faure. There is only one cinema, called Deepam's, in Victoria's Albert Street, but most hotels have in-house television and video.

During the day, Seychelles provides endless opportunities for such water sports as swimming, water-skiing, windsurfing, surfing, sailing, SCUBA diving, snorkeling, parasailing, power boating and big game fishing. Sports enjoyed by the islanders include soccer, basketball, volleyball, boxing and dominoes. Most events are advertised in the national press.

The interiors of the larger granite islands also provide a challenge for those keen to walk. The Ministry of Tourism and Transport has produced a series of ten small booklets entitled 'Nature Trails and Walks in Seychelles' which detail interesting walks around Mahé and La Digue. Copies are available at the Tourist Information Centre in Victoria's Independence House. If you intend to do some walking, these pamphlets are well worth buying, as they contain a mine of information about the buildings, vegetation and wildlife to be seen en route.

Flora and Fauna

Much of Seychelles' flora and fauna is unique. Most oceanic islands have flora and fauna that originally arrived over a long distance through dispersal by sea, wind or birds. Seychelles, however, still carries remnants and reminders of the super-continent to which it once belonged. The insect fauna, for example, is rich with Gondwanaland species, which have evolved into many different forms and continue to do so. These species have flourished because of the absence of predators. Trees and plants have evolved in many ways, too, some remaining close to African originals, others more related to oriental species, unheard of in Africa. Over time, however, these flora and fauna have developed unique characteristics and Seychelles' endemic species have arisen. For example, the *coco-de-mer* is found nowhere else in the world, as are several other species of plants and animals. Most of the 3,500 insect species in Seychelles are small and inconspicuous, with some notable exceptions. The extraordinary giant tenebrionid beetle, for example, is unique to Frégate and may be seen during the day resting on tree trunks. It is quite unlike any other insect, having a humpy back and spidery legs.

Seychelles is perhaps best known to birdlife enthusiasts for it shelters eight endangered species, 13 endemic species and a further 17 endemic subspecies. Some endemic birds, such as the black paradise flycatcher on La Digue, the black parrot on Praslin and the flightless rail on Aldabra are confined to one or two islands. However, less dedicated bird-watchers will probably find the very large numbers of nesting seabirds more spectacular than looking at individual birds. The most numerous, the sooty tern, nests in thousands on the islands of Desnoeufs, Bird and Aride. Another striking element of Seychelles fauna, before the early settlers exported or exterminated them in great numbers, must have been the giant tortoise. Now, the last great concentration of these strange creatures in their wild state is restricted to Aldabra which hosts 150,000 of them. In pens or small free groups, however, giant tortoises may be seen on many inner islands. Some are kept by hotels to interest tourists and some by families as pets. Other interesting animals include bats, lizards, chameleons and snakes.

Given its mid-ocean location, however, visitors may be more attracted to Seychelles' marine life than to its wildlife. The sea supports a much richer fauna than the land, sustaining several types of reef including atolls, fringe and platform reefs. There are more than 50 coral species off the main islands of Seychelles and at least 900 species of fish overall. Spectacular sea sightings include large schools of yellowfin and skipjack tuna, several species of whale — including the sperm whale which breeds in Seychelles waters — and bottle-nose dolphins. Four species of turtle are found around the islands, including the hawksbill and the green, all found on the most endangered animals list of the Convention on International Trade and Endangered Species (CITES). One

Common noddy tern on Aride Island (left). Endangered magpie robin found only on Aride and Frégate Island (right)

hundred and ten square kilometres of sea and sea-bed have been designated as national parks for the conservation of marine ecosystems. Virtually all fishing is prohibited in these areas and all corals, shells and other marine life have complete protection. The use of spear guns is totally prohibited in Seychelles. However, you may swim, snorkel, SCUBA dive and sail, but a fee may be levied on each person entering the perimeter of the park. Marine national parks include the waters in and around Baie Ternay, Port Launay and St Anne around Mahé and Curieuse and the gulf between it and Praslin.

As for flora, the most visible plants, because of their bright colours, are tropical flowering varieties such as bougainvillea, hibiscus and the sweet-smelling frangipani. However, along with trees, such as the breadfruit, casuarina and takamaka, they do not form part of the earliest vegetation of Seychelles. Originally the islands were covered by tall trees and palms. Huge timber trees formed an almost complete canopy from shore to mountain peak and nourished several endemic species. Such primeval vegetation is now found only in the higher, less accessible parts of Mahé, the upper slopes of Silhouette and the

White-tailed tropicbird nesting on Aride Island

Vallée de Mai in Praslin. An exception is the ancient mangroves which still dominate some areas of the coastal plateau, being the only land plants able to tolerate the salt levels and low oxygen content of the mud creeks.

Of 1,100 plant species present in Seychelles, about 75 are endemic. Without doubt, the most famous tree in Seychelles is the *coco-de-mer*, which in its natural state only grows on Praslin and Curieuse. It is possible, however, to see the tree elsewhere — in the Botanical Gardens on the outskirts of Victoria, for example. Two other interesting examples of endemic flora are the Seychelles pitcher plant and the jellyfish plant. The Seychelles pitcher plant is one of only two out of 70 species of pitcher plant in the world not found in the Orient. It is insectivorous and grows in isolated mountain recesses on Mahé and Silhouette. The jellyfish plant was believed extinct until recently when seven specimens were found in a high, inaccessible part of Mahé. An unusual, primitive shrub its fruit resembles a jellyfish. Hence the name.

Almost 50 per cent of all land in Seychelles is designated either as a national park, reserve or protected area. Two areas, Aldabra atoll and the Vallée de Mai on Praslin, are World Heritage Sites, protected under international law as unique natural sites of world importance. There are just over 100 such sites around the world. Three islands — Aride, Cousin and Aldabra — form special reserves, where flora and fauna are protected under Seychelles law.

People and Culture

It is almost impossible to define a 'typical' Seychellois. This colourful mosaic of people is the outcome of two centuries of inter-racial harmony between the different races that migrated to the islands from Europe, Africa and Asia. The result is a fascinating blend of racial features and skin tonings, through all the graduations of coffee, bronze and golden to the very palest complexions.

The first elements to arrive were European and African in the latter part of the 18th century. When they settled land allocated by the French Government, the French brought with them slaves from Madagascar and the African mainland. African slaves continued to arrive in the 19th century; some were smuggled in even after 1835 when the British Empire abolished slavery. In the 1860s, 'liberated Africans' seized from Arab dhows by British ships were released in Seychelles. It was also in the 19th century that small numbers of Indian and Chinese traders began to arrive. By sheer weight of numbers, however, it is the African influence which is now dominant in Seychelles society. The main European influence is French, recognisable not only in the

Creole language, but also in the food, culture and religion. The French introduced Catholicism, the religious persuasion of 90 per cent of the islanders. Seychellois women are avid churchgoers who consider going to church a social as well as a religious outing. However, to an extent the Catholic faith goes hand-in-hand with 'gris gris', an island form of black magic and superstition originating from African and Madagascan beliefs. In times of need many islanders may still consult a *bonnonm dibwa*, medicine man. The African influence is also detected in island music and dance, as well as in Kreol (Creole), the *lingua franca* of the islands.

Creole has evolved from the early settlement days when African slaves — from tribes with different vernaculars — and those from Madagascar had to adopt, and adapt, the language of their French masters to communicate with them and to have a common language between themselves. The written form is phonetic and consists mainly of words of French origin. Creole also contains some words of African, Arabic and Malagasy origin which give it both colour and charm. Most Seychellois also speak English and French, if only a little.

The Asian element can be noted in the island's cuisine but is particularly dominant in business and trade.

It is the islanders' broad-minded approach to love and romance that has really created this melting pot of people. Ask a Seychellois woman if she has a husband and she will most probably say 'yes'. In fact further questioning may well reveal that the couple have never been married and that he is not the father of any of her children, all of whom may have been sired by different men. These days, as in many parts of the world, one practical reason why couples do not get married is the expense which, given the large and lavish receptions which are part of Seychellois tradition, can be prohibitive.

As few couples marry, the woman, in very many cases, is the head of the family. Often it is she alone who raises and supports her children, with the help of an extended family unit. The number of births where no father acknowledges the child is high at 45 per cent. However, health care and education are free and social benefits generous.

In fact, the Seychellois have such a range of social benefits available if necessary that they have no compelling incentive to strive to improve their lot. Life has always been easy-going for the Seychellois. Blessed by a warm climate, they need few clothes and surrounded by one of the world's most plentiful seas, they need not look far for food. An old Seychellois saying has it that, 'if you go hungry, you are lazy'. As a result, indolence (not necessarily a bad quality) has become an almost innate characteristic of the people.

Certainly, the Seychellois believe life is to be enjoyed and like to have a good time. They love to dance and are naturally drawn to the beats and rhythms of their forefathers. Both the *sega* and the *moutya*, two of the most famous Seychelles dances, mirror traditional African customs. The sensual dances fuse two concerns central to African life — religion and social relations. Traditionally, the somewhat complex and compelling dance movements were carried out under moonlight, around an open fire to the rhythmical beat of the heated skin of a drum of African origin. The melodious *kontredans,* or country dance, on the other hand, was introduced by the early French settlers as a lighter form of traditional dance, something of a cross between a waltz, polka and berliner, rounded out to the accompaniment of a 'kamtole' band of fiddle, accordion and triangle.

Dances were regular events in village halls but have largely died out in recent years. That does not mean, however, that the Seychellois have stopped going out. Nowadays, they are more likely to be in one of the modern nightclubs, doing the *sega* on the dance floor and knocking back beers. A large number of the Seychellois are happiest when they have a drink in their hand. Even the botanical artist Marianne North recognised this in 1883. 'At Christmas and New Year the whole population

Opposite: Creole style house at Anse Takamaka.

The Seychellois are happy people, who believe life is to be enjoyed

got mad drunk. All the black and brown people began by going from house to house, wishing 'banana' or 'bonne annee', and in return got a glass of rum, or money to buy it. At night we heard singing and raving all round; it was like the island of lunatics, and we barred all the windows well before going to bed: to sleep was impossible.'

Combined with their *joie de vivre*, the Seychellois have a hospitable streak which is hard to match elsewhere in the world. The Seychellois are always welcoming, and friends — both old and new — are never turned away, should they pop round to a house for a drink or chat. Groups tend to gather on the verandahs of their houses, generally recognised as ports of call and centres of exchange. Perhaps because they never know who might stop by, the Seychellois keep their homes spick and span. Whether a house is a corrugated construction with a hard sand floor or the latest modern bungalow very much depends on a family's social status, but it does not affect how meticulously the woman of the house cares for it. Furthermore, the front yard, always well-kept, is usually overflowing with flowers. Large milk tins, sometimes brightly painted, are recycled as pots for flowers and medicinal plants and placed in line to create a welcoming entrance.

In general, homes play a highly visible part in maintaining traditional Seychelles life. Many old colonial houses are well preserved, although the indigenous palm-thatch may have been replaced by a corrugated iron roof.

While housewives are busy keeping the home clean, the men are likely to be out at sea fishing for their supper and perhaps a few extra fish to make some cash. Among the variety of boats used for fishing is the 'pirogue', the origins of which are thought to lie with the African dug-out canoe. Pirogues are traditionally tarred and painted black with white weatherboards. Excellent for launching off sandy beaches and rowing through surf, pirogues are often seen at Beau Vallon Bay where they are used for seine fishing — encircling fish with nets. The Seychelles schooner is a single-masted sailing craft, usually about 12 metres in length, which is taken out to sea on five- or six-day fishing trips.

For a nation that is only a little over 200 years old, the Seychellois have developed their own culture, one which, unlike many Western cultures, is not based so much on tangible objects such as buildings and works of art, but on a way of life. And despite emerging from so many varied backgrounds, the beliefs, behaviour and traditions of the Seychellois have fused to create a new society. One which, like the islands themselves, is unique.

1
VICTORIA

V ictoria, the capital and commercial centre of Seychelles, is the only town of any size in the country and is located on the east coast of the main island of Mahé. Eight kilometres across at its widest point, Mahé is 27 kilometres long and covers an area of 154 square kilometres. Almost 90 per cent of the islands' 75,000 inhabitants live on Mahé. Victoria has a population of 25,000, which qualifies it as one of the smallest capitals in the world. Lying in a well-sheltered natural harbour, protected by the islands of the St Anne Marine National Park, the town is backed by an impressive barrier of mountains. Looking up at these peaks from Victoria, Morne Seychellois is the one you see on the left. The highest point in Seychelles, its summit is 905 metres (2,969 feet) above sea level. The three peaks to its right are known as 'Trois Frères' (Three Brothers), the tallest of which rises to a height of 699 metres (2,293 feet), the third highest point in Seychelles.

The British captain of an East India Company ship, Alexander Sharpeigh, made the first recorded visit to what is now known as Victoria in 1609. Frenchman Lazare Picault also anchored in the bay during an exploratory trip to the islands in 1744. Twelve years later, Nicolas Corneille Morphey used the same excellent anchorage when he claimed the islands for France. When it was first settled in the late 18th century, the town was referred to as 'L'Etablissement de Roi' (The King's Settlement), which was normally shortened to L'Etablissement. In those early days, the inhabitants had to contend with a thick coastal band of mangrove swamp in which crocodiles abounded. By 1811, the settlement had expanded, thanks to an economic boom provided by the cultivation of cotton, to include about 100 small wooden houses with simple shingle roofs. In 1841, the town was renamed Victoria, in honour of the Queen of England. It is now known to the locals simply as 'town', as it is the only one in Seychelles.

In 1883, the botanical artist Marianne North described what then existed of Victoria. 'The little town with its trees and gardens is squeezed into a narrow valley, so that only the houses along the sea's edge were seen as we approached it over the long pier. On each side was a wide stretch of black mud and sand, covered with exquisite turquoise crabs with red legs, so beautiful that I dropped my bag and screamed with wonder at them, to the amazement of my porters, who said coolly they were not good to eat.'

In the Empire Review of 1930, E. Blackwood Wright detailed his entry into Victoria. 'Not only is the harbour safe and capacious, it is also very picturesque. As you enter, on the left are leafy, hilly islets with white cliffs and coral sands; on the right, and in the front, are the steep mountains of the main island, wooded to the top. Above the town that lies in the bay the white coral Government House shines out amongst the trees. All along the shores are villas embowered in bougain-villia, with a bright yellow bignonia covering their roofs, while their hedges are gay

Bird's-eye view of the port of Victoria, the Seychelles capital

with scarlet hibiscus. You land on a mole some half-mile long and planted with trees. After passing the Court House, once the Oriental Bank, a Carnegie Library, and the Club overlooking the football and cricket ground, you come to the gates of Government House, which is approached by an avenue of huge Dragon's Blood trees.'

Victoria has grown a little since those days, but not a lot and all the activity still revolves around the roads that stretch out from the Clock Tower or 'L'Horloge' — a replica of a clock on London's Vauxhall Bridge Road — which is now a national monument. Paid for by public subscription, the clock was raised in 1903 to mark Seychelles' new status as a British Crown Colony, separate from that of Mauritius. Originally black in colour, this silver clock has never chimed. It was supposed to, but when it arrived from London, after numerous delays, the pendulum was dropped over the side of the ship during unloading and lost. The engineer in charge of public works did his best to construct a substitute but the clock refused to chime.

The clock makes an ideal starting point for a tour of central Victoria, which is easier to view on foot, than by car. There are two central car parks, one on State House Avenue, the other next

The Clock Tower is the focal point of Victoria

to the Stade Populaire, the entrance to which is on Francis Rachel Street. A simple street map may be found in *Seychelles Rendezvous*, the free tourist magazine issued by the Ministry of Tourism and Transport.

However, if you intend to visit the large reclamation projects — mostly occupied by commercial zones — which have been built up since 1969, it is advisable to tour these areas by vehicle, particularly during the heat of the day, when walking longer distances may be tiring and, ultimately, uncomfortable. In fact, the heat makes it advisable to tour Victoria either in the early morning or late afternoon, but not too late as the town tends to close down soon after 5 pm when it appears deserted.

The road north from the Clock Tower is known as Albert Street, after Queen Victoria's husband (rather than Albert René, the present President of Seychelles). On the left-hand side at the beginning of this street, is Mahé Trading Building, which houses, on the first floor, the headquarters of Travel Services Seychelles, one of the main travel agents and tour operators on the islands. Continue along the road and over the St Louis River, which is little more than a drainage sluice, and Mahé's main taxi rank is on the right, shaded by flame trees. Previously the town's bus station, it has always been a place where people stop to while away their time, swapping idle gossip. In the early 20th century, it was the rickshaw stand — an old photo (now available on postcards) may be seen in the bar of the Northolme Hotel in the north of the island. The taxi rank is the starting point for number four 'Beau Vallon-Victoria' in the series of 'Nature Trails and Walks in Seychelles'.

Next door to the taxi rank is Camion Hall, home to one of the CODEVAR shops known as 'Artizan de Zil'. A non-profit organisation established in January 1991 to promote traditional craft industries in Seychelles, CODEVAR sells a wide variety of craft products including 'vakwa' bags and hats made from the fibre of one of the islands' endemic palms, as well as some innovative creations such as ceramic and coconut jewellery. All the products have one thing in common — they are genuine souvenirs produced to a very high standard from Seychellois raw materials and designs. Camion Hall also houses several craft shops including Seychelles Creations, selling jewellery, buttons and hairclips made of natural fibres, and Kreol d'Or which produces 18-carat gold jewellery using Seychelles symbols such as palm trees, coconuts and fish.

Opposite Camion Hall, the recently renovated office block of

Premier Building has several modern boutiques on the ground floor. Further along the road stands the largest supermarket in Seychelles, belonging to the Seychelles Marketing Board (SMB), as well as a whole array of old emporiums, offering a wide variety of goods for both locals and tourists. Jivan Imports, on the corner of Albert Street and Market Street, is probably better known than the rest, simply because its proprietor, Kantilal Jivan Shah, is a legendary figure in Seychelles.

Known simply as Kanti, he is an amateur biologist, historian, anthropologist, masseur and cook. In an interview with one of England's national newspapers he also described himself as a 'bullshitter'. But that would be to underrate him. Kanti has done a great deal to gather information about the history of Seychelles and his 'library' (a huge jumble of magazines and books) contains much valuable information about the country — most of which is already stored in his head. Kanti has also been a staunch guardian of the country's environment. His work in this field earned him the silver medal of the Royal Norwegian Society of Sciences and Letters, as well as a United Nations Environment Protection 'Global 500' award. Some credit must go to him for the statutory protection of flora and fauna in the islands.

Kind and friendly a fellow as Kanti is, entry into his shop is likely to turn into an invitation to his flat above the shop, lunch or supper, a massage with essential oils or at the very least, a palm reading session — particularly if the caller is a pretty young woman. Primarily, however, Kanti is a merchant and his shop sells everything from cloth and books to sarongs and music cassettes attracting a mixture of both locals and tourists. Barclays Bank which offers a foreign exchange service, faces Kanti's store.

Carry on along Albert Street, past Deepam's Cinema (the only one in the country) until the T-junction. There take a right turn and the town's bus station is located on the left-hand side. Buses carry passengers from there all over Mahé from early morning until early evening. Take a left turn at the T-junction near the cinema into Oliver Maradan Street and the Roman Catholic Cathedral of the Immaculate Conception, which was built in 1898, is on the right.

The cathedral is famous for its clock, which chimes twice — just before the hour and again on the hour — and was immortalised by author Alec Waugh's book *Where the Clocks Chime Twice*. No one is quite sure why the clock chimes twice, but the trick has spurred many a story such as . . . 'It is a mistake that was never rectified' or 'It was designed that way for the local population — the first chime in order to wake them up, the second to tell them the time'. It has even been suggested that, like certain Swiss clocks, it chimes twice to give busy business people a double check.

During weekdays, the Cathedral is quiet, but on Sunday it comes alive with people decked out in their smartest clothes. Youngsters preparing for their First Communion stand out from the crowd, dressed as they are in all their finery. Even after mass, there is plenty of activity, with christenings carried out at the end of the service. Afterwards, couples pose proudly for photographs with their babe in arms. The light-hearted nature of these families, their laughter and their smiles, is always striking.

Next door to the cathedral is the Capucin Seminary, a national monument, built in 1933 in a Portuguese architectural style. Local and foreign friars live there, some of whom teach in the island's primary schools. A beautiful stone building next door to the Seminary, constructed earlier this century, is now the Seminary's printing works.

Carry on along Olivier Maradan Street (named after a former Roman Catholic Bishop) which leads into St Joseph Street to return to the centre of town — or take a right turn along Hangard Street (named after the most successful early settler) to view one of the older residential areas of town with its typical Seychellois houses and traditional general stores — stocking everything from brooms, baked beans, clothes and curry powder to perfume, pins, spoons and spirits. Take the first road right into Button Lane and continue for about half-a-kilometre to watch Guy Cesar recycling old wooden furniture into beautiful boxes, of all shapes and sizes, the lids of which are inlaid with bold geometric designs created from different kinds of wood and mother-of-pearl. He also makes backgammon sets and chess boards to order. All the finished products are polished with beeswax and oiled to Guy's secret formula, which includes cinnamon oil, and smell divine. His boxes are on sale in various outlets throughout the island, including Camion Hall in Albert Street. Backtrack to Hangard Street, turn right and located at the end of this road, is Spectra Studio Designs, one of the largest producers of souvenir T-shirts on the island. Visitors are welcome to watch the handmade production of various designs.

Return to the centre of town by taking a left turn along Labourdonnais Street. Where this road meets Revolution Avenue, there are several late 19th-century shops. Typically, the upper floors of these stores serve as the shopkeepers' homes. Turn left down Revolution Avenue past Belonie School, a primary school previously known as St Louis College (one of the first schools in the country, when it was established in 1867 by the Roman Catholic Marist Brothers), is on the left-hand side of the road. Education in Seychelles is free and compulsory between the ages of six and fifteen — the majority of children also attend crèche from the ages of four to six.

Several traditionally-styled houses are set back from this road. One building near the corner of Revolution Avenue and Quincy Street is now a shop. When it was built in the 19th century it became the first government maternity hospital on the island. The original stone wall — blocks of coral cemented together with a mixture of red earth and lime — still exists but, unfortunately, it has been plastered over.

Along Quincy Street, named after Chevalier Jean-Baptiste Queau de Quinssi, the influential French administrator of Seychelles from 1794 to 1811, Christy's art gallery stocks a wide range of work by local artists, including Serge Rouillon, Elizabeth Rouillon, Christine Harter, Michael Adams, Donald Adelaide and Egbert Marday. Some are little more than crude prints, but there are many original watercolours and oils. Further

Brightly coloured traditional-style house on Mahé

along the road, a recently built Hindu temple stands.

Take the first right into Market Street, probably the busiest street in town with many emporiums and arcades, and the Sir Selwyn Selwyn-Clarke Market (named after a British governor of colonial days) is about 100 metres down on the right-hand side. The original market opened in 1839, when Seychelles was still a dependency of Mauritius, which considered the interests of the smaller territory secondary to its own. Requests for money to build a market were refused, and the Civil Commissioner of Seychelles was told to approach 'the more wealthy and public-spirited inhabitants' to pay for the building, on condition that they would be repaid later with dues from the market. Eleven years after the market opened, those public-spirited inhabitants were still petitioning Mauritius to reimburse them from market dues, only to be told that they should consider it a speculative investment which failed to pay off. They never saw their money.

The best time to visit the busy, bustling market is early on a Saturday — it opens every day at 5:30 am — when activities tend to pick up as people are free from office duties to stock up their larders and the market is lively and loud. People greet each other across the stalls and haggle over the price of fish while the white cattle egrets — known locally, but no one knows why, as Madanm Paton — strut gracefully around the market, unperturbed by all the noise and fuss.

Visitors who enter the market through a proud archway bearing the market's full name are greeted by a colourful array of stalls sheltered by beach umbrellas. Piled high with fruit and vegetables, these stalls provide an insight into the indigenous food of the islands. Tomatoes, green peppers, onions, lettuce, cucumbers, carrots and green beans lie side by side with the more exotic 'sousout', which has a pale green, spiky skin and 'patole', which is similar to a cucumber but is hollow inside. Over all this, lies the pervasive smell of fish, and it is the fish stalls, immediately at the left on entering the market, that attract the most attention. Mackerel, tuna, barracuda, snapper, parrotfish, octopus and shark can often be found there — it much depends on the catch of the day. The essential final touches to a local meal, spices and chutneys, can be found in the market.

Fruit is also in abundance. Aside from the more common pineapples, mangoes, papaya and watermelon there are unusual, seasonal attractions to search out such as 'santol', a fairly tasteless fruit encased in a hard, furry capsule, and golden apple or 'frisiter', a hard green fruit used mostly in salads, or 'jamalacs', recognisable by their white or bright pink conical shape.

Not only food is on offer. There are fascinating curios, such as pestle and mortars, as well as more traditional souvenirs such as locally crafted jewellery and knick-knacks. A small florist's sells sprays of orchids, which are grown commercially in Seychelles for export to Europe. Fibrous coconut husks are also on sale. Islanders use these husks to polish their floors. Rather than kneeling down and scrubbing, one foot is used to manoeuvre a coconut half across the floor, producing movements not unlike those of the local *sega* dance.

Exiting the market by the main entrance on Market Street, take note of the men who sit across the road, carefully weighing and rolling tobacco from their wooden boxes, tailoring their 'cigarettes' with a personal touch, as in the old days.

Turn right and a little further along Market Street, there is a boutique called Sunstroke Designs, which sells good quality, innovative clothing and accessories for the tropics that have all been locally designed and hand printed. Upstairs, there is an art gallery displaying original paintings, etchings, batiks and prints by a range of local artists. Almost opposite Sunstroke Designs is Church Street where Brijals Trading print personalised T-shirts, shirts and caps using any photograph which they are given — be it a photo of Madonna or a favourite holiday snap.

Backtracking along Market Street, take the first left after the market into Benezet Street, a lane which leads past a traditional barber's shop and several general stores to Revolution Avenue. When you reach the avenue, Mason's Travel, one of the main tour operators, is on the right while on the opposite side is the Central Police Station.

It has stood on this site since the early 19th century, but the present building was opened in 1950 by Sir Selwyn Selwyn-Clarke. In days gone by, the Police performed a number of tasks not normally associated with the force, including the supervision of Crown Lands, taking the official census, operating the local postal services, quasi-military duties, and checking and numbering thousands of palm trees licensed for the production of toddy. The Chief of Police was also public prosecutor, inspector of liberated Africans and Sanitary Inspector for Seychelles.

Turn left down Revolution Avenue and St Paul's Anglican Cathedral is on the right. Built in the 1850s, it was consecrated as a church in 1859 by the Right Reverend Dr Ryan, Bishop of Mauritius, who travelled to Seychelles specially for the event. Before land was reclaimed this building was on the seafront. The church, which has since been extended considerably, became a cathedral in 1973. Given that Anglicans are a minority in Seychelles, it is small by European standards. In complete contrast, the most popular nightclub on the island, The Love Nut, on the ground floor of Premier Building, is situated opposite.

A walled alleyway between Central Police Station and the Anglican Cathedral leads, via a public car park, to State House Avenue. On reaching the end of this short cut, look to the right for a view of the State House gates and a glimpse of its grounds.

State House is closed to the general public, but permission may be given to visit State House Cemetery, a national monument, where several important figures in Seychelles history, including de Quinssi, are buried. State House, an impressive colonial building, is similar in style (perhaps not surprisingly as they were both constructed in 1904) to the old National Library (which is opposite), but much larger. It is said to have been designed by the wife of a former governor early this century who realised, after building had begun, that she had forgotten to put any staircases into the plan!

The former National Library, another national monument, used to house the country's library which moved to a new build-

State House and its verdant gardens overlook Victoria

ing on Francis Rachel Street in 1994. The first floor of the old library accommodated the reference section, as well as a selection of fairly up-to-date foreign newspapers for those starved of international news.

At the corner of State House Avenue, close to the Clock Tower, Victoria House accommodates both the American Embassy and the British High Commission. Turn right at the Clock Tower into Francis Rachel Street. The area on the left is reclaimed land.

On the right, at the entrance to Victoria House shopping arcade which is known as Passage des Palmes, Temooljee's, one of the largest and oldest stores in Victoria, sells household goods and foodstuffs. Inside the arcade, a bookshop and knick-knack shop called Antigone, offers a wide selection of books on Seychelles, as well as local maps.

Some of the oldest Indian shops, such as Adam Moosa and Chaka Brothers, owned by families who have lived on the island for generations, are further along Francis Rachel Street. Opposite is the only petrol station in town.

Next door to the building that houses the King Neptune takeaway stands the restored building which accommodates the Seychelles People's United Party (SPUP) Museum. The SPUP (now known as the Seychelles People's Progressive Front) came to power as a result of a *coup d'état* in 1977. This area once contained one of Seychelles' most popular hotels, known, like the woman who ran it, as 'La Princesse'. The hotel also functioned as a brothel and when customers realised that the Seychellois gave freely of their love, the hotel failed. La Princesse was subsequently declared bankrupt and died in poverty.

Further along Francis Rachel Street, between the Habib Bank and Chaka Brothers store, is an unsignposted lane known as 'Rue de la Poudrière', (Street of the Powder-Magazine), which was the site of the islands' first ammunition store. The Possession Stone, claiming Seychelles for France in 1756, is also thought to have been laid in this area. Just beyond the narrow street a driveway leads to the country's only Islamic Centre and Mosque.

Opposite, in front of the 'Stade Populaire' (Popular Stadium) is Fiennes Esplanade, a shady promenade to which to retreat from the midday sun. The Stade, the largest in the country until the completion of the new National Stadium in the summer of 1993, has been the setting for many occasions and events, including the swearing-in ceremony of James Mancham, the first President of Seychelles, when the islands gained independence from Great Britain in 1976; Liberation Day (5 June) parades, the date of the *coup d'état* in 1977; sporting events; and the mass celebrated by Pope John Paul during his visit in 1986. Next door to the stadium is the impressive new building of the Seychelles National Library.

Across the road stands the striking headquarters building of Cable and Wireless where attractive and unusual phone cards for the many public phones around the island may be bought and international calls placed. The splendid old-style Kenwyn House beside it, painted in white and blue, is a national monument. It is the home of the Cable and Wireless manager. Constructed around 1868, it was purchased by the telephone company in 1894. The name was a common one used by Cable and Wireless for their managers' houses in various parts of the world.

Near the end of Francis Rachel Street, the upstairs of a contemporary building set back from the road houses the studio that supplies Sunstroke Designs. It is possible to watch various products being made and to obtain goods at a slight discount.

At the end of the road, the 'Le Chantier' (The Yard) roundabout, as the French name suggests, was once the boat-building and woodworking centre of the town. The national monument in the centre of the roundabout, erected in June 1989, is known as 'Monument Linite' and portrays sailfish, which symbolise unity. Take the exit to the right, Mont Fleuri Road, which is the old east coast road and head south towards the airport.

On the left-hand side is a car hire company. Opposite it stands National House, which used to be known as The Secretariat in colonial days. It now accommodates several departments of the Seychelles Government. Beyond the first turning on the right, known as Liberation Avenue, is the Pentecostal Assembly, while Avis Rent A Car is on the left. Take the turning opposite the new buildings of the Ministry of Environment, Economic Planning and External Relations, built in old colonial style, to enter the Botanical Gardens. The car park is immediately on the right.

The gardens, protected from development by their status as a national monument, cover about six hectares (15 acres) and are an excellent place for a cool stroll after the heat of the town centre. The gardens were laid out in 1901 by Paul Rivaltz Dupont, a Mauritian Director of the Botanic Station, and then the Botanic gardens themselves, until 1934. He travelled to the East in 1902 and 1911, returning with exotic species, in particular, the 'useful' plants of the tropics. The collection then boasted 20 types of banana, fruit and spice trees such as star fruit, durian and cola, and 26 varieties of palm.

The gardens remain of interest today but few trees or shrubs in the gardens are labelled. A pamphlet guide is available from the kiosk at the entrance. Some of the plants, however, are easily recognisable. For example, an ashok tree — tall, straight and slender — stands at the car park entrance, while on the far side grow magenta-coloured catkins of red hot cats' tails. The cascades of scarlet-flowered fountain bush, with its feathery leaves, and a brassy yellow cassia tree, are also easy to pick out in the area.

Several species of palm, flanking the driveway, include one small talipot palm on the right. This primitive tree flowers after 60 years and then dies. There are sisal plants, with rosettes of large, sharp, silver-green leaves, on the left, and, in front of the Ministry of Health building halfway up the drive on the right, several small, squat palms. These are fully grown Round Island bottle palms, the pygmy of the palm world which is endemic to Round Island, Mauritius.

Continue up the road where a bed of flowers is often a mass of colour with red ginger, the aptly named shrimp plant, poinsettias and the fiery-orange peacock flower. Believed to be from South America, the lacy peacock flower no longer exists in a wild state. Just beyond this bed, the Giant Tortoise pen has a female *coco-de-mer* tree in front of it.

Fabulous tales surround the giant tortoises of Seychelles, which, until the advent of the early settlers, roamed wild on the islands. Now the only remaining natural population is on Aldabra. Early accounts mention the large number of tortoises as easy prey for both sailors and settlers.

In 1609, aboard the first ship known to have reached the granitic islands of Seychelles, John Jourdain wrote that 'the boat returned and brought as many land tortelles as they could well carrie. The tortelles were good meat; but after two or three meales our men would not eat them, because they did looke so ugly before they were boyled.'

Giant tortoises live to a grand old age, as has been noted in the past. In 1766, an expedition took five to Mauritius and in 1828, Admiral Sir Henry Keppler noted that one which was housed in the grounds of Government House in the Mauritian capital of Port Louis, could move 'with six men on its back, three each side, standing on the edge of its shell, holding hands across'. Colonel Fredrich Fair ended the story of this remarkable creature when he wrote that 'the tortoise . . . mentioned in 1828 by Henry Keppler died at Fort George in 1918, after falling 12 feet and breaking its neck.' The battery notebook suggested that it had

Brightly coloured Mokara Madame Pannes orchid

Giant tortoises, which are only found in their natural habitat in Seychelles and Galapagos, can be seen in Victoria's Botanical Gardens

committed suicide 'on hearing that Fort George was to be manned by the local Volunteer Force'.

Another amusing tale details the plight of Jonathan, an ancient tortoise from Seychelles housed in the grounds of the Governor's residence on St Helena. When Jonathan took to disrupting croquet games on the front lawn by sitting on the balls the governor put out a plea for a prospective mate, about 140 years old with a sense of humour. During a playful fit, Jonathan had pushed his last mate over a cliff.

Enough of myths for now. The elephant apple tree, easy to distinguish if it is in fruit, is a little further up the hill from the giant tortoise pen, on the lawns to the right. The tree's large, hard, green, round fruits have a slight, rubbery aroma. Another tree easy to spot when it is in flower is the octopus tree, which has a striking, large inflorescence like the tentacles of an octopus. Nearby, freshwater pools sprout pretty water lilies and large-leaved taros. The drumstick tree to the left of the pools produces a seed with a long stalk, topped by a rounded ball of anthers.

Crossing the lawns takes one to the far right of the Botanical Gardens where stone steps ascend to the Sapin Restaurant and Snack Bar, located in a picturesque spot underneath towering Norfolk and Cook Island pines. Close by, a number of banyan trees, with their aerial roots growing down and their tangled roots forming natural steps, give a wild, jungle feel to the area.

Descend by the opposite set of steps to pass by one of the strangest plants in the world. The tall cannonball tree bears waxy, red flowers on short, woody stalks directly from its trunk, and the cannonball-shaped fruit it develops lends the plant its name. On the edge of the grassy area a cola tree reveals its source of the ingredient for that famous drink. Bear left towards a rough track, pass over a small stream and you will arrive at a striking monument unveiled as a symbol of Japanese–Seychellois friendship in 1991. Return along the same track and reach the road which leads to the car park.

After a tour of the Botanical Gardens, turn left at the main entrance and Mont Fleuri Road will lead you back to the Le Chantier roundabout. The right-hand exit, Latanier Road, leads down to the New Port. Maison du Peuple, a striking red Praslin granite building at the beginning of Latanier Road and another national monument, is the headquarters of the SPPF.

In front of the Maison du Peuple, Bois de Rose Avenue leads off to the right. Built on reclaimed road, this east coast road provides a fast route to the airport and the south-east. Flamboyant discotheque, one of Seychelles' top night spots, is located 200 metres down on the left-hand side. The only other landmarks along this road are the national stadia of international standard built for the 4th Indian Ocean Games, held in 1993.

Return to the Le Chantier roundabout and take the exit known as 5th June Avenue, past a model of an Air Seychelles aeroplane and on the right there is a large children's park, complete with big boating lake, built in 1989. The entrance to the Seychelles Yacht Club, a popular watering-hole for island residents is a little further along the road. The Marine Charter Association next door represents the many owners and skippers whose boats are available for big-game fishing, day cruises or longer charters to the distant islands. On the opposite side of the road stands a metallic sculpture called 'Zomn Lib', another national monument commemorates 5 June, the SPPF Party Day, which shows a man snapping a chain of bondage in two.

Carry along 5th June Avenue to a roundabout which features at its centre the national Bicentennial Monument, designed by Italian artist Lorenzo Appiani. It was erected to mark 200 years of settlement on the islands. Known to the locals as 'Twra Zwazo', it symbolises the three elements of Seychellois ancestry: Europe, Africa and Asia.

The road right leads to the older of the town's two piers, known as Long Pier and the Inter Island Quay. The local tuna canning factory is located on the Old Pier — tuna is the second T on which the Seychelles economy is based, the other is tourism. The tuna industry has witnessed spectacular growth in recent years. Canned tuna exports, which began in 1987 with the establishment of a joint French-Seychelles tuna cannery now account for well over half of all physical exports which, however, still only account for eight per cent of foreign exchange. The Inter Island Quay, as its name implies, is the point from which local schooners deliver cargo and passengers to the outlying islands of Praslin and La Digue. Le Marinier restaurant is located at the pier and is a great place to watch the comings and goings of the port, while enjoying a drink or meal.

The 5th June Avenue continues north from the opposite side of the roundabout and heads along the east coast to the settlement of Anse Etoile.

Turn left at the roundabout and the focal point of Victoria, the Clock Tower, is once again straight ahead. Before reaching this national monument, however, on the left Independence House accommodates several government departments and, on the ground floor, the Tourist Information Office. Next door to the centre is L'Amiral, a popular restaurant among those interested in a simple meal or a leisurely coffee and snack. The ground floor of Independence House also accommodates a survey office which sells good ordnance survey maps of various Seychelles islands. The grim, grey building beside Independence House houses the Central Bank of Seychelles.

In Kingsgate House on the opposite side of the road there are several souvenir shops including Oceana Studio, the offices of British Airways and Air France, Kim Koon offering a one-hour Fuji film processing service (usually about 4 hours in practice), and the National Travel Agency another of three large tour operators. Through the car park next door Gordon Square may be glimpsed. The square was created in 1862 when a large landslide swept through Victoria killing nearly 100 people. The 'square', which is so named after General Gordon, is now used for various sporting activities.

Another shopping arcade back on the left-hand side of the road houses more souvenir shops, as well as Kodak agents Photo Eden, which provides a one-hour film processing service, and photographic and water sports equipment. Just beyond the arcade, the Pirate's Arms, which used to be a hotel, is now a restaurant, cafe and the most popular meeting place in town. The French Cultural Centre is located on the first floor.

Close to the Pirate's Arms, another branch of Barclays Bank offers foreign exchange facilities, and Lakaz Boutique des Artisans (craft shop) and many outdoor stalls sell a wide range of souvenirs such as T-shirts, shells and turtleshell jewellery, which tourists are not encouraged to buy. Turtles and tortoises go through agony when their shells are removed. The shell has to be removed when they are alive as it is too difficult to remove once rigor mortis has set in. Importation of turtleshell is illegal in most countries around the world because it is the product of an endangered animal.

Behind the stalls, outside the elegant colonial building of the Law Courts, stands a monument to Queen Victoria which was donated by Britain to mark the 40th anniversary of the coronation of Queen Elizabeth II (2 June, 1993). It replaced the original which was placed there on 5 January 1900 commemorating the sixtieth anniversary of Victoria's reign. Around the corner is a bust of Pierre Poivre, a national monument erected by the Sey- chelles Society in 1972 to remind Seychellois of their debt to this botanist-cum-statesman, Governor of Mauritius when Seychelles was still a dependency of that country, who introduced various spices to Seychelles in the early days of the colony. Later, from the 1930s up until the 1980s, together with copra cinnamon became one of the two most important export cash crops.

The National Museum, on the opposite side of Independence Avenue is a national monument, and was originally the Carnegie Library, built with funds from the Carnegie Trust. It is guarded by patina-covered cannons, discovered in 1971, of the Falconet, or swivel gun variety, which represented a significant advance in fire power in the early fifteenth century. Well preserved, they carry the Royal Coat of Arms of Portugal, as well as the emblem of King Manoel I. The Possession Stone, laid in 1756 by Nicolas Corneille Morphey to claim French ownership of the islands, is also now in the Museum, as are old documents listing slave arrivals on the islands, exhibits of indigenous flora and fauna, such as *coco-de-mer*, shells, birds, butterflies, crabs, corals and a grossly deformed piglet.

Victoria's post office is next door in Liberty House. Seychelles is famous for its stamps, which are among the most beautiful in the world. Given the unique flora and fauna, fine beaches and exotic subjects which the islands boast and which are frequently depicted on local stamps, this is hardly surprising. Sets of stamps are extremely popular souvenirs for tourists.

Additional Information

Christy's Art Gallery
Quincy Street
Victoria
Tel: 321 019
8am to 4:30pm Monday to Friday
8am to 12noon Saturday

National Library
State House Avenue
Victoria
Tel: 321 072
8:30am to 5pm Monday to Friday
8:30am to 11:45pm Saturday

Botanical Gardens
Mont Fleuri
Tel: 224 868
6am to 6pm every day

Tourist Information Office
Independence House
Victoria
Tel: 225 313
8am to 5pm Monday to Friday
9am to 12noon Saturday

National Museum
Independence Avenue
Victoria
No telephone
8:30am to 4:30pm Monday to
Friday
9am to 12noon Saturday

General shopping hours
Victoria
8am to 5pm Monday to Friday
8am to 12noon Saturday

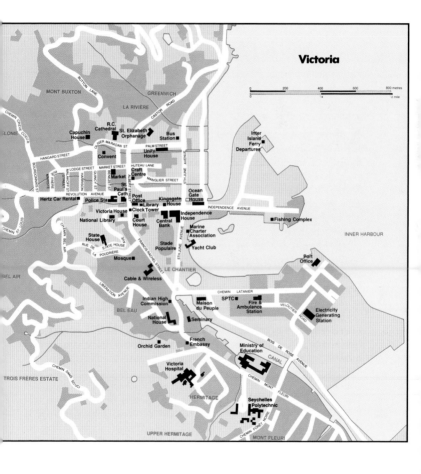

Victoria

0   200   400   600   800 metres
0   ¼   ½ mile

MONT BUXTON
GREENWICH
LA RIVIÈRE
BUTTON LANE
CASTOR ROAD
CHEMIN CREVE COEUR
ELONIE
Inter Island Ferry Departures
R.C. Cathedral
St. Elizabeth Orphanage
Capuchin House
Bus Station
OLIVER MARADAN ST
PALM STREET
HANGARD STREET
Convent
Unity House
5TH JUNE AVENUE
Market
Craft Centre
LODGE STREET
MARKET STREET
HUTEAU LANE
MAYGLIER STREET
BOURDONNAIS ST
MAHE FRERE
MALMERT ST
HARRISON
QUINCY ST
BENEZET ST
ALBERT STREET
St. Paul's Cath
Hertz Car Rental
Police Sta
REVOLUTION   AVENUE
Post Office
Library
Kingegate House
Ocean Gate House
INDEPENDENCE   AVENUE
Fishing Complex
Victoria House
Clock Tower
National Library
Court House
Central Bank
Independence House
Marine Charter Association
State House
STATE HOUSE
RUE   DE   LA   POUDRIÈRE
Stade Populaire
FRANCIS RACHEL STREET
5TH JUNE AVENUE
Yacht Club
INNER HARBOUR
BEL AIR
CHEMIN BEL AIR
Mosque
LE CHANTIER
Port Office
LIBERATION   AVENUE
Cable & Wireless
Indian High Commission
BEL EAU
CHEMIN LATANIER
SPTC
Maison du Peuple
Fire & Ambulance Station
VELOUTIER ROAD
Electricity Generating Station
National House
Seminary
French Embassy
Orchid Garden
Ministry of Education
BOIS   DE   ROSE   AVENUE
CANAL
CHEMIN SANS SOUCI
TROIS FRÈRES ESTATE
Victoria Hospital
CHEMIN MONT FLEURI
HERMITAGE
Seychelles Polytechnic
CHEMIN FORET NOIRE
UPPER HERMITAGE
MONT FLEURI

2
NORTH OF VICTORIA

Most visitors to Seychelles are familiar with a part of northern Mahé, if only because of Beau Vallon, one of the most famous of the island's 68 beaches. The north of the island, however, has much more to offer to those willing to investigate. From Victoria to North Point (via Anse Etoile), the road leads past the National Archives at La Bastille, the only perfume house in Seychelles at North East Point, and a host of residential districts which hug the wild north-eastern coast and secluded northern coves. Also en route are a number of guesthouses and restaurants, should refreshments become a necessity. For the adventurous, a rough track leads from Pointe Cèdre over the hill to Glacis, just north of Beau Vallon; for the energetic, this track follows one of the 'Nature Trails and Walks in Seychelles'.

Heading south to Beau Vallon from North Point there are two interesting artists to visit: Vladimir Tarakanoff in Glacis and Ron Gerlach right on the beach at Beau Vallon. There are also a number of small hotels on the way, including the Northolme, an old haunt of such writers as Ian Fleming, Somerset Maugham and Alec Waugh. It has more charm and character than most hotels on the island. Several of the larger hotels front the beach at Beau Vallon. Most operate watersport centres from which it is possible to indulge in a little SCUBA diving, water-skiing or parasailing. A side trip from Beau Vallon along the coast to Bel Ombre and Danzil leads to the start of another of the routes detailed in the 'Nature Trails and Walks in Seychelles' series.

The studio of Italian sculptor Antonio Filippin is just off the main road from Beau Vallon to Victoria. En route, make a short diversion to Le Niol to visit Gordon's pottery workshop, and soon after the road leads into the suburbs of the capital. On nearing the centre of Victoria again, take the twisting Sans Souci hill road to reach Port Glaud on the west coast of Mahé. En route, are the starting points of several heavily forested hill walks in the 'Nature Trails and Walks in Seychelles' series, several good viewing points and the country's only tea plantation where a tavern offers a welcome and, after all this driving, a well-deserved cup of tea.

The route around the northern section of Mahé starts in Victoria. From the roundabout which intersects Independence Avenue and 5th June Avenue, marked by the Bicentennial Monument, head north along 5th June Avenue. Almost immediately, the road crosses the St Louis River, Gordon Square is on the left, the reclaimed land of the Long Pier on the right.

The first side road is Manglier Street, which wends its way to Albert Street in the older, market area of town. Continuing along 5th June Avenue, the road crosses Moosa River, and there is another side road known as Palm Street. This leads back into the northern end of town close to the Roman Catholic Cathedral of the Immaculate Conception.

Still on 5th June Avenue, pass the Central Bus Terminal on the left and the School Meals Centre (SMB) on the right. The English River Clinic is on the left and a school with basketball court and football pitch — soccer is considered the national sport — is on the right.

About 200 metres after the Palm Street turning, you come to a small row of shops with parking facilities. The first building, Boston House, accommodates Samy's store (a general store), Ram's Car Hire and Chez Xavier (a hairdressing salon). The building next door houses the Krishna Mart, with general foodstuffs downstairs and shoes, clothes, material and some household goods on offer upstairs. A bakery and another general store are located in a third building.

Looking inland at this point, the impressive granite faces of 'Trois Frères' (The Three Brothers) and Morne Seychellois are clearly visible, towering above Victoria. Out to sea, the St Anne Marine National Park and St Anne, the largest of all the islands located in the park, lie majestically offshore. The view may well be marred by an inverted triangle of red slats; a landing approach marker to Seychelles International Airport, further south along the east coast.

Continue along the coastal road to the English River Community Centre and the English River District Council buildings. English River, a residential suburb of Victoria is of little interest except as a mix of modern housing, an occasional traditional Seychellois house and some typical general stores. To visit English River, turn into Castor Road, which almost doubles back on 5th June Avenue. There are two call boxes at this junction — a card phone and a coin phone. Castor Road reaches its conclusion back in town, close to the Roman Catholic Cathedral of the Immaculate Conception.

Back on the east coast road (a continuation of 5th June Avenue), the headquarters of the Seychelles Broadcasting Corporation's radio station (SBC) are located just after the Castor Road turning. Next door to the SBC is the Livestock Development Agricultural Promotion Division Veterinary Services, Union Vale and the Pest and Disease Control Services Office.

The Union Vale Industrial Estate is on the seaward side of the road, another SMB building is on the left and the Sunshine Furniture Workshop is on the right. The rest of the buildings on this road are predominantly residential.

About 1.5 kilometres from the Bicentennial Monument, on the very promontory from which the area of Pointe Conan derives its name, is an impressive three-storey stone building, fronted by a wrought iron fence and gate. It is a national monument, known

Paraglider takes to the sky from Beau Vallon Beach

as La Bastille, and it houses the National Archives. Designed by a
Swiss-German and built in the 1930s, La Bastille was originally a
family home. According to local legend, when Jean-Baptiste
Jumeau acquired the home (near Anse aux Pins) which now
houses the Lenstiti Kreol and renovated it for his son, his daughter complained that she had received nothing. Jumeau duly had
La Bastille built for her. Its name derives from the fact that it was
only built with one door and, when viewed from the sea, it resembles a prison. After it ceased to be a family home in the
1950s, it housed a succession of government departments before
being handed over to the National Archives in 1989.

Just inside the gates of La Bastille, a sculpture by Tom Bowers
in the centre of a small lily pond depicts three famous traditional
Seychellois musicians with their instruments. There are various
large scale models of machines in the garden, including a rope
maker, copra mill, sugar cane mill and coffee peeler, all housed
in traditional thatched stalls. There are also some interesting old
pictures of these machines in use, but unfortunately all the captions are in Creole, so visitors have to either use their
imagination or find a friendly islander to translate.

On display in the entrance hall inside the National Archives
building is a rickshaw (used in Seychelles earlier this century)
and, in a room to the right, a permanent collection of island art

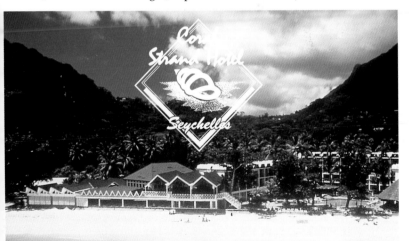

by local artists. Those who want to see it need permission from the staff in the research room, located upstairs. The research room also has some interesting old photographs and paintings. One 18th century map of Seychelles was presented to the National Archives by Brian Baldock, chairman and managing director of Guinness, in February 1992. A Seychellois family tree follows the line back to the mid-18th century and provides a fascinating insight into the inter-marriage between island families. Other exhibits include an old picture of Victoria's port area; a diagram of the carvings on the front of the Possession Stone as they appeared originally; a painting of an estate house at Anse à la Mouche and an old photograph of Victoria around 1919 in which State House, as it is now known, is about the only recognisable man-made feature. The research room also contains old documents on Seychelles, newspaper files and a reference library.

While the National Archives concentrate on all matters relating to Seychelles history, the small house tucked behind it is the National Heritage Centre — a valuable source of information on all cultural aspects of the islands.

Leaving La Bastille, the coast road continues north past a traditional, green-painted building housing Saravanar Store, a general store, with open views across the St Anne Marine National Park on the right-hand side. Shallow water and underlying corals cause the sea to reflect many different hues of green and blue, broken only by the granitic outcrops that rise from the ocean.

Just past the Saravanar Store a left turn leads to the Seychelles Institute of Management (SIM), a government institute at Ma Joie, which offers intensive management courses to those who have already made their mark in the world of business. Many lecturers are from overseas.

The Twilight Disco, popular with both locals and visitors, is on the right-hand side of the east coast road, as is Le Surmer Hotel and Restaurant, which has just eight spacious, clean, well-furnished and fully air-conditioned rooms. There is a great open-air restaurant, with unobstructed views over the water. On the opposite side of the road, the Sea Breeze which is a Relais des Îles, has just six rooms.

The two general stores in the centre of Pointe Conan — Jova's and Pillay — both retail goods, tobacco and liquor. Note that there is always a place for a licence number on the boards displaying a retailer's intent, but that there is never one present.

The next area along the coast, known as Ma Constance, is

reached when the Far Eastern Broadcasting Association (FEBA) building displaying the motto — 'The World of Life, at the Speed of Light' — comes into sight. FEBA beams Christian messages to many Far Eastern countries, hence the large number of aerials rising from the shallow waters offshore. There are two more general stores in the vicinity. The Calypha Relais des Îles, located a little further along, has just three rooms.

Anse Etoile, a relatively large settlement along this stretch of coast, has its own Bahai Centre and police station, which has a barrier (normally raised) in front of it. The single call box outside the police station takes coins only. The card call box is on the opposite side of the road. 'Anse', as you have probably realised by now, means a small bay, cove or beach, but the literal translation, from old French, is the semi-circular handle of a pot or basket.

The village also boasts the only Japanese restaurant on the island, called Kyoto. Soon after, there is a general store known as Digwaz Boutique, housed in a modern building. There are parking facilities outside, so it is easy to pull in for a cold drink and a light snack. Elderly men often sit beside the store, in a large shady area where they play — with great gusto — dominoes, a national sport almost as popular as soccer.

Nearby there is another general store and then the road cuts through the playgrounds of Anse Etoile School, where volleyball, basketball and football are all on offer. Perched on high, just next to the school is the small church of Saint Antoine de Padua. It is quite likely that this was built to replace the first chapel ever built on Mahé, in 1787, which was also dedicated to Saint Antoine de Padua, but no trace of the original chapel remains.

Rounding the bay of Anse Etoile at Pointe Cèdre, the Manresa Restaurant and Guest-house is built on reclaimed land. This small establishment of just five rooms provides excellent views of Victoria harbour and the St Anne Marine National Park and is recommended to those with limited budgets.

Opposite Manresa a steep road which leads uphill is only for those who are prepared for a little adventure and who do not mind missing the spectacular scenery of the northernmost tip of the island, or doubling back to take it in. Far from being a main road, the twisting, often extremely steep and sometimes rough track, which, at best, has two concrete strips to mark the route, is about as far off-the-beaten track as you can get in a car on Mahé. Far from the white sand beaches that attract all the tourists, this is where small island life continues undisturbed.

Where the road starts to climb, it passes the Foyer de Nazareth, an orphanage started in 1965 by Father Maurice Roh. Modern houses are surrounded by immaculate gardens, the red earth of which produces rich greenery. One or two small houses built in traditional style are raised up on rocks. In the old days, these houses were built almost entirely of wood or had a wooden frame with walls made from the fronds of palms and a roof of thatched palm. More recently, corrugated iron has been used for both walls and roofing. By raising the house up on rocks, the builders helped to preserve the wood and palm from termites, flooding during the rainy season, and also to ventilate the house better and keep it cool. It is a type of house which is fast disappearing in favour of modern concrete or stone structures.

The capital's water comes from the La Gogue reservoir, opened in June 1979, which is close to the highest point of the road. And yet, even after reaching the reservoir the road still climbs steeply skywards. When the brow of the hill is finally negotiated, the descent to the west coast of Mahé presents stunning views across the water to the outlying island of Silhouette, which is easily recognisable by the almost omnipresent cloud which seems to sit above it. Lower down, the road passes through a new housing development, built by a Malaysian corporation and completed in June 1991. There is a public coin phone box within the development. Soon after, the track meets the main coastal road at Glacis. Take a left turn there to travel on to Beau Vallon Bay or double back on your tracks to return whence you came.

Back at Pointe Cèdre the east coast road continues north past Etoile de Mer, a restaurant located on the land-locked (left-hand) side of the road, which serves Creole and continental cuisine, specialising in seafood. Parking facilities for clients are provided on the opposite side of the road. Rated in a Ministry of Tourism survey as one of the best restaurants in Seychelles, Etoile de Mer serves local food in an exciting and innovative way. Such dishes as chicken stuffed with skipper lobster are unlikely to be found anywhere else.

To the right, all along this coastal road there are picturesque views out to sea, but particularly on the stretch north of Etoile de Mer. The road is built right out into the sea, and offers excellent, open vistas of St Anne Marine National Park, only slightly marred by the antennae of FEBA which rise out of the sea.

On the corner where the road bears left to follow the natural course of a wide bay, there is another general store, with a call box outside. To most islanders the bay is known as 'Smelly Corner' for rubbish dumped into the water since the 1970s to reclaim

There are many secluded beaches on the north coast of Mahé.

land — which has never been reclaimed — creates a strong and unpleasant smell. Rounding the northern end of the bay, the road passes a shop housed in a modern whitewashed building. Silvie's sells clothes geared more to the local market than the tourist.

Opposite the shop, some 100 metres further along the road, are the ruins of two lookout posts built by a small British army contingent, based at Anse Etoile during World War II.

The east coast, particularly this north-eastern section, is wild when compared with the rest of Mahe's coastline. The reef, marked by crashing waves, is very close to the shore. Inside the reef, the sea is calm and shallow, and coral beds are visible under the water, even from the road. Islanders often wade there — sometimes waist deep — looking for octopus to fill tourists' plates, but as it is impossible to swim in this area it is not popular with tourists.

Located in a stunning beach house along the straight stretch of road that borders Anse Nord d'Est, Kreolfleurage Parfums is also the home of Pit Hugelmann, the creator of the perfumes, and his family. German by birth, but now a naturalised Seychellois, Pit spent two years researching and testing, before launching his first perfume, an exotic scent called 'Bwanoir'. It was so successful that the flowery 'Bambou' and the spicy 'Ambre Vert' followed hot on its heels. The next fragrance, for men and only available in Belgium, will be called 'Takamaka'. In future Pit will concentrate on natural medicines and aromatherapy products, particularly for the British market.

✱ The Kreolfleurage perfumes are all made from natural ingredients, using over forty flowers and plants such as jasmine and ylang-ylang, as well as a host of other secret components that give a distinctively Seychellois fragrance. An added attraction of the perfumes is their presentation. The bottles are in local wood containers, each one individually crafted by hand.

These unique perfumes may be purchased direct from Kreolfleurage Parfums or from several shops around the island, including the Airport Duty Free Shop. They are also marketed as an exclusive product in England, Germany, Belgium and Singapore.

Continuing north, the road passes through a small village where just before a sandy football pitch on the right, there is a coin-operated phone box. The North Point Hospital is on the inland (left) side of the road, as is the Rehabilitation Centre, opened in 1982 to help the seriously disabled by providing physiotherapy and speech and occupational therapy treatment.

Leaving the north-east behind, the road rises along the northernmost section of Mahé, passing Carana Beach, a beautiful sandy cove surrounded by giant granite boulders. Driving through the district of Machabée, many of the beautiful houses on the ocean side are hidden from the road by lush vegetation. From a boat out at sea, however, they appear to cling precariously to rock faces, while the sea crashes dramatically below.

There are many small, quiet, secluded beaches in this area. Unfortunately, however, although no beach in Seychelles is private, access to some of them is restricted because the land around them is private.

Soon after Machabée and its single general store, the entrance to Les Manguiers, which is a small guesthouse composed of two houses and just four bedrooms is on the right-hand side of the road.

Among a profusion of Spanish-type villas along the left-hand side of the road is the majestic entrance to Villa Falcon, owned by a wealthy Arab. On the right, the North Point Guest House, with eight, clean and fairly well maintained rooms, is situated on a small promontory, tucked out of sight behind a copse of trees. It is here, opposite the tiny island of L'Îlot (North Islet), that the road swings back south along the west coast.

The district of Glacis begins beyond a coin-operated call box to the right. Glacis is also the name of the dramatic granite rock faces that are such a common feature of Seychelles. Up a side road is Chez Jean, a small guesthouse with five spotlessly clean air-conditioned rooms all with top-quality furniture. Two public phone boxes — one coin and one card operated — are close by.

Another coin-operated call box is next to Chetty's Fancy Store. Turn down a track just opposite the store and you arrive at a small beach tucked away behind the vegetation where there is unlikely to be another soul.

Carry along the main road, past the Glacis District Council building, outside which there is another coin-operated call box, and a basketball court. Close to the sea is Mancham's old house, now abandoned.

A pedestrian bridge over the road marks the location of the 37-room Vista Bay Club. The walkway joins the popular Danielle's Restaurant, which offers a variety of Creole, Chinese and international cuisine in a setting overlooking the sea to the right, with the main section of the hotel on the hillside to the left. The hotel's air-conditioned rooms all have a minibar and television set. The swimming-pool is for the exclusive use of hotel guests.

From here continue south along the coast road to the Glacis Health Clinic and the Church of Saint Jean-Baptiste, which is dedicated to St John the Baptist. The first church in Glacis, a thatched wooden building, was erected in 1882. Eleven years later, the stone church was completed on the present site and renovated in 1934 and 1993. If you are lucky, you might catch sight of the pair of Seychelles kestrels that often nest in the belfry. There is a statue of St John the Baptist holding a cross in the grounds of the church and, on the right-hand side of the church, a small man-made grotto dedicated to the Virgin Mary, in which a few pews are drawn up in front of a statue of the Madonna. Just behind the church, set in lush and extensive gardens, the imposing colonial-style presbytery completed in 1936, is where the priest lives.

Next to the church is the end of the rough track that leads over the hill from Pointe Cèdre. This is where walk number two 'Glacis-Anse Etoile' in the 'Nature Trail and Walks in Seychelles' series begins, leading hikers back up the minor road and over the hill to the east coast. Almost opposite the church is Glacis Police Station. Continuing south along the western coastal road, there is a general store and two call boxes, one for cards, one for coins.

Beyond this, the Sunset Beach Hotel is located on a small promontory known as La Blache. All 25 rooms, 17 deluxe rooms, six junior suites and one villa, have sea views and sea-facing patios, which provide a great setting (predictably, given the hotel's name) to watch the sundown. The junior suites are particularly appealing as they occupy the end of the rocky peninsula while the villa has prime position at the top of the promontory. The secluded beach, reached by a pathway from the hotel, provides ideal conditions for snorkeling. Big-game fishing trips may also be arranged by the hotel. Other facilities include a swimming-pool, sundeck, gym, video room, boutique, restaurant serving international and Creole dishes and bar, while a shady terrace overlooking the beach is a perfect setting for afternoon tea.

Back on the coastal road, not far from the Sunset Beach Hotel, is Vladimir Art Studio. There is no signpost; this studio is the first house after the Cable and Wireless telephone exchange building on the coastal side. Cars must be left at the top of the drive and from there it is a steep walk down into the magical

The Sunset Beach Hotel on the La Blache promontory

world of Vladimir Tarakanoff and his wife Claire-Lise. Now a Swiss national, Vladimir was born of Russian parents in the former Yugoslavia. While studying at a Swiss art school in the late 1960s, he met a young Seychellois woman whom he decided to drive home in a camper van. After four months of adventure in Europe, the Middle East and Africa, they arrived in Seychelles, where Vladimir, enchanted by the islands, lived until 1978. In 1991, the lure of the islands brought him back to Seychelles from Brazil where he had set up shop in the years between. His desire to 'live with nature' led him to his house-cum-studio. A small, ramshackle place, it is a brightly-coloured home of considerable charm. The azure sea crashes reassuringly on coastal rocks some 100 metres away, and the surrounding vegetation is packed with countless animals including a giant tortoise, hundreds of birds attracted by the constant supplies of rice and a lizard which always appears for its daily helping of cheese.

As expected, Vladimir's art is as full of colour and character as his life. His streets of Victoria and beautiful beach scenes burst with vivid hues of watercolour and gouache. Although the majority of his clients are tourists who prefer the beach scenes, local residents and some visitors who have been coming to the islands for years, favour the paintings that depict Victoria in the good old days. Vladimir paints them from sketches that he drew when he lived in Seychelles in the 1960s and 1970s. He also produces some abstract acrylics, but he says 95 per cent of his clients prefer the Seychelles scenes. Quite unusually for a Seychelles artist, all his paintings are originals. He does not sell prints and his originals are only available from his house.

The Northolme Hotel is located 100 metres from Vladimir's home-cum-studio for those prepared to battle across country, or a few minutes by road for the less adventurous. The Northolme is an institution in Seychelles for it is the oldest hotel on the island, pre-dating the opening of the airport in 1971 when the modern tourism boom began.

There is a great deal of history attached to the quiet, secluded lodge. Noel Coward, Somerset Maugham and Ian Fleming were all inspired to write when they stayed there, and one of the erotic Emmanuelle films with Sylvia Kristel was filmed there. An old-style hotel, small and friendly, it boasts few modern facilities other than 19 air-conditioned rooms and a SCUBA diving centre — some excellent dive sites may be reached from the hotel's beach — but the homely atmosphere cannot be matched by any other hotel. The bar is well worth a visit, even for non-residents, because it is full of sepia photographs of Seychelles in days gone by.

Further south along the coast road, Vacoa Village, marked by the multi-coloured crazy golf course outside, is a self-catering establishment built in Mediterranean style, featuring 11 apartments, a restaurant, swimming-pool and bar.

Continuing south, Exoticars, a car rental company, is on the left, as is a general store. This marks the northern end of the kilometre stretch of Beau Vallon, the equivalent of Hawaii's Waikiki or Rio's Copacabana, which is a beautiful beach providing good swimming conditions. During the south-east monsoon (May to September) it tends to be as calm as a mill-pond, while for the rest of the year the north-westerlies whip up waves.

Beau Vallon Bungalows, a guesthouse offering six self-catering rooms, is located nearby. It may be close to the most popular beach on the island, but it is also near a marshy area at the mouth of the Mare Anglaise River and is damp during the heavy rains. Baobab's Pizzeria, on the right of the road, is popular with both locals and visitors — for good reason. While sipping an ice cold beer, clients can watch their pizza being prepared in the open oven with one eye, while using the other, in the evening, to watch the sun descend. The fact that the restaurant fronts Beau Vallon and its floor is a sandy continuation of the beach helps to generate a relaxed atmosphere, where, by Seychelles standards, it is relatively inexpensive to eat.

Next door to Baobab's is a diving club called 'Les Diables de Mer' (The Devils of the Sea) and opposite is La Fontaine, a casual restaurant which serves seafood, local Creole dishes, snacks, fast food (curries and typical English dishes such as fish and chips) all day long. There are two call boxes outside the restaurant — one for coins, the other for cards. Next door is the Beau Vallon Shopping Centre which sells snacks, ice cream and souvenirs, including postcards and stamps.

A little further south the Boat House fishing centre offers big-game fishing, as well as day trips to Silhouette. Big-game fishing, with lunch and drinks thrown in, costs around SR3,000 for a full day and SR2,000 for half a day, per boat. Day trips to Silhouette, which include the use of snorkel equipment, a tour of the island, lunch and drinks cost SR500 a person (children are free). Big-game fishing facilities are also available on the journey over to the island, if clients are interested. The centre operates two boats *Yellowfin* for six & eight people and *Bluefin* for four people. The Boat House also sells miniature models of boats.

On the beach opposite the Boat House is Ron Gerlach Batiks studio and shop. Now a Seychellois citizen, Ron arrived in Seychelles in 1969 to work as a structural engineer on the construction of the Coral Strand Hotel and what is now known as the Vista Bay Club. Once these two projects had been completed, however, he turned to his great love in life — the production of batiks. Seychelles happens to be an ideal place in which to practice this art form as all the necessary ingredients are readily available — pure silk and cotton are imported from China and India, beeswax is an island staple, cool clear water pours down the mountain streams and the equatorial sun is strong enough to dry and fix the colours. Producing a batik involves a long and difficult process. The design is first drawn on pure white cotton or silk, then wax is applied to the parts of the material that are not to be dyed. Each colour is applied separately to the fabric and as wax and dye build up on the material, some cracking of the wax may occur, resulting in the trademark lines that litter a genuine batik. The islands have proved to be a great inspiration to Ron. The enchanting bird life, fascinating underwater world and daily island life are faithfully reproduced on his handmade dresses and shirts, as well as beachwear, scarves and pictures.

At the back of Ron Gerlach Batiks, the coast road divides into the old and the new. The road which curves to the left, away from the beach is fairly recent. Follow it and take the first road to the right which leads to a convenient parking area for those who wish to spend a few hours whiling away their time on the beach. Alternatively, carry on along the new road until a right-hand turn giving directions to La Perle Noire restaurant is encountered. Turn right and follow it to the end where there is another parking lot, closer to the Beau Vallon Bay action.

Alternatively, those travelling by foot from Ron Gerlach Batiks may either walk along the beach towards the centre of Beau Vallon Bay or continue along the old coast road which has been sealed off to vehicles and has round concrete seating built on it. At the northern end of this 'promenade', next to the Batiks studio and shop, is the Tropicana discotheque, which is also called the Beau Vallon Beach Pub and Sea Grill, as well as the Paradise Nightclub.

Continue along the promenade, enjoying the cool sea breeze and the distinctive view out across Beau Vallon Bay to the island of Silhouette. Pass the remains of a coconut plantation, a few basic beach huts and public toilets, to arrive at the Buvette Hibiscus

Restaurant, which is open every day except Monday. Shaded by the many trees that edge Beau Vallon beach, it is an ideal place to eat *al fresco*.

The Underwater Centre (Seychelles), a Five Star PADI dive centre out of which some of the most experienced dive masters in Seychelles operate, may be seen from the Buvette Hibiscus. A one-day introductory SCUBA diving course is available which consists of lessons in the swimming-pool in the morning, followed the same afternoon — if the instructor considers the student to be competent — by a dive in open water. A five-day PADI open water dive course, resulting in a full diving licence on completion, is also offered. For qualified divers, an excellent range of dive sites with coral gardens, caves, shark banks and granite boulders are easily accessible from the Centre.

The dive centre is attached to the Coral Strand Hotel, a four star hotel, which occupies one of the best hotel locations in Seychelles, right on the beach, in the centre of the most popular bay. One hundred and two double bedrooms, all with bath/shower, airconditioning, telephone, relayed music/radio and balcony accommodate the guests, who may enjoy meals either in the main restaurant or by the pool and sundown drinks at the poolside bar. During the day, a large number of watersports are on offer, including windsurfing, minisailing, surfboarding, water-skiing, parasailing, water scootering, catamaraning, snorkeling and the amusing 'water sausage'. Evening entertainment is provided in the form of local dance shows, and fashion shows and a disco from Wednesday to Saturday. On Sunday evenings, most of Mahé seems to descend on the Coral Strand to enjoy the hotel's legendary happy hour. There is also a casino located a five minute walk away, at the Beau Vallon Bay Hotel.

Near the main entrance to the Coral Strand Hotel, the La Perle Noire restaurant, open seven days a week for lunch and dinner, advertises itself as being 'world famous', but that claim is difficult to authenticate. La Perle Noire is said, however, to be one of the two most popular restaurants in Seychelles — the other being La Scala at Danzil. Reservations are recommended.

Continuing along this small access road, away from the beach and back towards the main road, there is a coin-operated phone box and a general store on the left. Papillon Souvenir Boutique is little more than the front room of somebody's house which has been opened to sell souvenirs. Opposite is a signpost to Villa Napoléon, a two-house establishment with a total of six rooms. The Coco D'Or guesthouse has 25 rooms and a restaurant and bar which are open to non-guests during the evening.

On reaching the main road, take a right turn and follow the road to a T-junction, on the corner of which is Beau Vallon Police Station. The St Louis Road to the left, leads back to Victoria, while the one to the right goes to Bel Ombre and beyond, terminating at Danzil.

Turning right into the Bel Ombre road, there is a tiny house on the left-hand side whose walls are made entirely of metal boxes, hammered flat and stuck together. One hundred metres from the T-junction is the entrance to the Beau Vallon Bay Hotel, one of the oldest and most popular hotels on the island, given its excellent location right on the beach. The hotel has 122 air-conditioned rooms, all of which were renovated in 1993, three restaurants serving a mixture of Creole, Chinese, Italian and international cuisine and two souvenir shops. There is a swimming-pool, tennis, volleyball, table tennis, watersports such as parasailing, water skiing, sailing and windsurfing and a dive centre where the headquarters of Marine Divers International is located. This is a five star facility offering tuition in PADI and NAUI methods, in several different languages. A wide number of courses are available, ranging from basic introductory courses to advanced

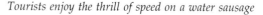

Tourists enjoy the thrill of speed on a water sausage

instructor levels. Up to four dives are conducted by Marine Divers daily — they visit more than 30 different sites, on coral reefs, boulders and wrecks. Evening entertainment provided by the hotel includes local bands, traditional dance shows and discos. The entrance to the Casino des Seychelles is located in the hotel lobby.

Back on the Bel Ombre road, roughly 700 metres from the entrance of the Beau Vallon Bay Hotel, is the 'Polytechnique des Seychelles Ecole', a hotel training school. Members of the public may enjoy Creole-influenced meals at La Goélette restaurant where the food is prepared by students. The restaurant is open for lunch from Tuesday to Friday and for dinner on Wednesday, Thursday and Friday.

Just over a knoll, the Fisherman's Cove Hotel, situated at the southernmost end of Beau Vallon Beach, is managed by the French Le Meridien hotel group. With only 48 rooms, this exclusive hotel has been built using traditional building materials such as granite, timber and palm thatch. Facilities include a swimming pool, tennis courts and, of course, the beach. The one restaurant serves both Creole and international cuisine, while local song and dance shows are staged several times a week.

Just past the Fisherman's Cove, it is possible to glimpse Bel Ombre beach through the trees. The beach is more popular with locals than with tourists, probably as it is less accessible and, as a result, much quieter. Opposite a coin-operated call box, surrounded by green lawns, lies the Church of St Roche. The interior decor is very simple — just one mural behind the altar, while the windows lack any stained glass and are merely louvred. Its exterior, however, makes it one of the most attractive churches on the island and it may be seen, casting a watchful eye on all the bay's activities, from any point on Beau Vallon. Its tranquil atmosphere and graceful architecture contribute to an ethereal effect that is lulling, particularly when the late afternoon sun bathes its yellow painted walls.

Further along the road, Bel Ombre School boasts a red-earth basketball court. Opposite is Harold's Store, a general store, and the Bel Ombre Video Centre. Several establishments in this area offer accommodation, including Daniella's Guesthouse, Le Tamarinier Restaurant and Guesthouse (a small, moderately priced hotel with 11 rooms and an intimate restaurant specialising in seafood), and the Bel Ombre Holiday Villas, a four unit self-catering establishment. Bel Ombre is also home to another general store outside which are two call boxes, one for cards, one for coins; a football pitch; and the Russian Ambassador.

Le Corsaire restaurant on the right, is built out into the sea and serves a mix of international and Creole cuisine. The restaurant's name means 'pirate' and is so called because there is believed to be pirate treasure buried nearby.

The story of the search for treasure goes way back to 1730, the year that Olivier Le Vasseur — known as 'La Buse' or 'The Buzzard' — was led to the gallows in Réunion for fourteen years of piracy. One of the most notorious pirates ever to operate in the Indian Ocean, La Buse, along with the English pirate John Taylor, captured the Portuguese ship *Vierge du Cap* in 1721 when it lay helpless after a storm in the port of Bourbon. She was laden with great treasures. Part of the booty was the legendary Fiery Cross of Goa, a gold crucifix inlaid with diamonds, rubies and emeralds, so large and heavy that it required three able-bodied men to carry it. Pursued by the British navy, the pirates went into hiding, Taylor fleeing to Cuba and La Buse remaining somewhere in the Indian Ocean. It was not until 1730 that La Buse was captured, tried and sentenced to hang. Legend has it that, just as the hangman put the noose around his neck, La Buse took a piece of paper covered in symbols out from his clothing and threw it into the crowd, crying 'Find my treasure, he who can!'

Reginald Cruise-Wilkins, who came to Seychelles from Kenya in 1949 to recover from malaria, chanced upon a copy of La Buse's symbol-covered paper and spent the next 27 years working on the riddle, which he was convinced would lead him to buried treasure at Bel Ombre. Cruise-Wilkins died in 1976, having found only antique flintlocks, marbles and porcelain figures in the area, but his son John has been continuing the search in the same area, convinced that his father was right and that La Buse's treasure is to be found at Bel Ombre.

The end of the road is reached not far from the treasure excavation sites, which are clearly visible on rocks close to the right-hand side of the road. La Scala, the second of what are said to be the two most popular restaurants in Seychelles, is located up a flight of stairs. The restaurant, which serves a combination of international and Italian cuisine, is an excellent alternative for an evening out — the only time it opens. The setting is romantic, the service by Seychelles standards very good and the food, particularly the freshly made pasta, delicious.

A narrow secondary road continues up the hill, past the Danzil mini-market (a general store) to the badly-signposted Studio Oceana on the left. One of the oldest craft workshops on the island, Studio Oceana produces batik clothes and paintings to sell in its three outlets: Oceana Studio in Kingsgate House, Victoria, a shop in the Beau Vallon Bay Hotel and another at the Reef Hotel. Visitors are welcome to look around the workshop where ten people work as printers and dyers, while David Hoareau, the 'artist in residence', creates the batik paintings. If the manager of the Studio, Agnes Arnephie, is on duty, it is also possible to buy goods direct from the factory.

The entrance to the Auberge Club des Seychelles is almost opposite Studio Oceana. It offers 49 air-conditioned rooms, most of which are individual bungalows, landscaped into a terraced hillside. Facilities include a restaurant specialising in both Creole and international cuisines, a disco, traditional song and dance nights, swimming pool and boutique. The hotel does not overlook a good beach, but there are excellent snorkeling facilities around the rocks directly below the swimming pools.

After the Auberge Club the road peters out and becomes nothing more than a trail, details of which are given in booklet number one 'Danzil-Anse Major' of the 'Nature Trails and Walks in Seychelles' series. Roughly, the trail follows the rocky coastline of north-west Mahé, leading to the secluded beach of Anse

Tranquil setting of the Catholic church at Bel Ombre

Major (also known as Anse Jasmin). Much of the trail lies within the Morne Seychellois National Park and therefore offers spectacular 'glacis' (rock slopes) and interesting endemic vegetation. The two kilometres to Anse Major, which take about one-and-a-half hours to complete, have to be retraced.

Given that the road is a dead end for vehicles, backtrack to the T-junction next to the Beau Vallon Police Station. Travelling back along the Bel Ombre road, admire the mountains that rise up ahead and note the valley through which the road passes back to Victoria. Pass the Beau Vallon Police Station and follow the St Louis Road up the hill. There are several shops on this stretch of road, including: the Beau Vallon Supermarket (a general store), a Barclays Bank branch, Sunstroke (a branch of the store found in Victoria's Market Street), and Macouti (a gift and curio shop accommodated in an old traditional house). Just past Macouti there is a petrol station, the last one before Victoria.

Continue along the road, slowing down for the double hairpin bend and on the right-hand side a sign reads 'Sculptor Studio The Yellow Gallery Antonio — 100 metres, parking'. A very rough track leads to the home and studio of Antonio Filippin, an Italian who moved to Seychelles with his family in 1992. His large and impressive sculptures, most of them abstracts, are made mostly of wood, although he sometimes uses local granite or coral as well. Antonio's impressive old house is painted yellow, hence the name of the permanent gallery space, which he accommodates within his home and in which he features the work of local painters.

Returning to the St Louis Road, follow the twists and turns past lots of breadfruit and jackfruit trees, as well as several residential properties. Just beyond a boutique called Coco Zerm, there is a signpost to Le Niol, as well as one to Gordon's Pottery. Turn into this side road and bear right where the road forks, about 100 metres from the main road. Gordon's Pottery, run by Gordon Robert, is about 400 metres along the road. Gordon has been a potter for more than ten years and has operated his own business from his home at Le Niol since 1990. Prior to becoming a potter, he was a coxswain on a fishing boat but, unhappy with the lengthy trips away from his home and family, he decided to give it all up for a job on land. A good friend, who was teaching at a pottery co-operative called Seypot, noticed Gordon's artistic talent and suggested that he give pottery a try. Gordon trained and worked at Seypot for five years, until deciding to run his own workshop where he would have more creative freedom. Assisted by just one other potter, Gordon produces 100 different items, many of which incorporate familiar Seychelles symbols like the giant tortoise, *coco-de-mer* and fish. He makes simple designs such as ashtrays, as well as more complex pieces like tea-sets, the teapot of which will be shaped like a tortoise. Prices range between SR10 and SR650. Aside from his studio, Gordon's work may be bought at the CODEVAR outlet in Victoria's Camion Hall, the curio and book shop Antigone and the Duty Free Shop, but it is cheaper to buy at his workshop.

Opposite Gordon's Pottery, the Le Niol Guesthouse, a small, five-room establishment serves both Creole and continental cuisines in its restaurant. Continue along Le Niol Road, past some impressive private residences, and the road eventually peters out into little more than a red-earth track. From there, there are sweeping views across the whole of Beau Vallon Bay. Backtrack to the junction, close to St Louis Road, take a right turn and follow the road, through the residential district of Bel Air where the Russian Embassy is located, until it joins Sans Souci, the road that connects Victoria to Port Glaud on the west coast of Mahé. Otherwise, take the St Louis Road towards the capital. On the brow of the hill, right in the middle of the small residential area that is known as St Louis, is a general store. Mein's Car Hire is also located in St Louis.

Shortly after the road starts to descend, a right-hand hairpin bend offers panoramic views of Victoria. TBG Traders, a general store, is on the right and before another sharp bend to the right. Two public call boxes, one for coins, the other card-operated, stand close to the St Louis District Council office. Two general stores — one run by T M Pillay and the other called Siva's Shopping Centre — are on the same side of the road as the modern monolith of the Embassy of the People's Republic of China. Opposite, stands the Seventh Day Adventist Church at the front of which there is a plaque bearing the words 'Fear God and Give Him Glory', dated 1981.

Before the suburbs of Victoria are reached, there are two more large bends in the road, the second of which has a public housing estate to its right, and a general store. The well-known restaurant, Marie-Antoinette, is up a steep side road to the left called Serret Road. Marie-Antoinette, named after Louis XIV's mistress, is accommodated in a beautiful traditional house set in its own gardens. The house was built early in the 20th century, according to Madame Fonseka, the restaurant's septuagenarian proprietor, who remembers moving into the still quite new house when she was a young girl. Madame Fonseka has lived there ever since and has become something of an institution in Seychelles cookery circles since she opened her house to the public. Born and bred in Seychelles, she taught herself how to cook, because, quite simply, she had to. There were ten hungry children to feed. According to Madame Fonseka, an authentic Creole meal should include at least a curry, grilled fish, chutney and salad. However, to ensure that all the influences on the local cuisine are included in Marie-Antoinette's set menu (there is no à la carte), restaurant patrons are likely to find themselves sampling all that and more. A typical set menu includes aubergine fritters, grilled red snapper (African influence), tuna steak in Creole sauce, parrot fish in batter (European influence) and chicken curry (Indian influence), as well as salad and rice. And a meal in the friendly, homely atmosphere of Marie-Antoinette would not be complete without a coconut sorbet, a local favourite. Madame Fonseka also runs the Hill Top Guesthouse, located just behind Marie-Antoinette. This modern establishment has eight rooms, all with their own private bathroom or shower, and a restaurant which serves both international and Creole cuisines. The Guesthouse is well situated, close to town and the central bus station from where it is easy to pick up transport to any point on Mahé. It also enjoys great views across Victoria to the St Anne National Marine Park.

Four hundred metres down the hill from Marie-Antoinette, on the right-hand side, is the turn into the Bel Air Road which becomes Chemin Sans Souci and leads over the hill to Port Glaud on the west coast. Mahé's oldest cemetery, on the left-hand side behind a high wall, is a gloomy, sinister and rather overgrown landmark. It is the last resting place of the islands' first white (according to the law of the day) settlers. Among the interesting graves is that of the pirate, Jean Francois Hodoul, which has the inscription 'Il fut juste' (He was a good man). Just behind his tomb is the last resting place of Jean-Baptiste d'Argent, who was the brother-in-law of Seychelles' most famous administrator, Quinssi. The Giant's Tomb commemorates an early inhabitant who is thought to have been more than 2.7 metres (almost nine feet) tall. According to legend, he was so strong that even as a boy he could easily pick up a 'pirogue' and carry it down the beach to the sea. He could also pick up a sack of rice with his litte finger and it was generally reckoned that he had the strength of six men put together. However, according to legend, the other islanders became so afraid of his strength and what he might do with it, that they poisoned him in the 1870s. Another grave with an interesting inscription is that of a young British naval officer who died fighting a fire on board his ship. On the opposite side of the road, the stream that runs down from the hills forms pools which have long been used by the local women for washing their clothes. The clothes are then laid out, either on the grass or the headstones, to dry.

All the area to the right of the road, which is predominantly residential, is known as Bel Air. Take care 400 metres beyond the cemetery, for there is a sharp, double hairpin bend. 'Trois Frères' and Morne Seychellois are straight ahead as the road climbs the hillside. A lane to the left leads past the back entrance of State House and finally joins Poudrière Lane in Victoria. Opposite this lane is the Pension Bel Air. This seven-room guesthouse is housed in the old traditional-style family home of the Rassool family. One of the family, Roland, still manages the Pension. All the rooms are clean and well maintained and some have air-conditioning. Definitely in its favour are the elevated views over Victoria and the proximity to town. Victoria is a mere five-minute walk away thanks to the short cut down Poudrière Lane.

On the left-hand side the northern end of Liberation Avenue, a residential road, leads through the area known as Bel Eau. Just 100 metres along the road, there is an excellent panoramic view of Victoria where it is fascinating to ponder on the fact that most of what lies in front was once sea — successive land reclamation projects have greatly increased the size of Victoria.

There is a phone box on the corner of Liberation Avenue; behind which the new buildings of the Bel Eau School are clearly visible. It is at this point that the Bel Air Road becomes Sans Souci, which is known for its incredible twists and turns — take care! The road passes a general store called Rajan's Store, the Bel Air Supermarket — run by SMB — and a large white cross, and around a hairpin bend a traditional house, with lawns laid down to the road, is to be found.

Higher up the hill, a sign to the Residence of the British High Commissioner indicates the road that leads back to Le Niol. On another sharp corner, there is a right-hand drive to Mountain Rise Hotel and Restaurant. This five-room establishment is set on a small hilltop and thus affords excellent views of Victoria, its suburbs and the St Anne National Marine Park. Within the well-maintained gardens, there is a swimming-pool.

The higher the road climbs, the smarter the houses, although many of them are hidden from view behind impressive gates and

Sandragon trees haunt the trail to Mahé's old hillside mission

long driveways. One such residence is that of the American Ambassador, who lives in the house to which Archbishop Makarios of Cyprus was once exiled. During his time in Seychelles, the archbishop was well known for two eccentricities. One of them was climbing — fully robed in black vestments — to the summits of the Morne Seychellois range; the other was singing old Greek folksongs as he sat on the front lawn at the end of the day surrounded by fellow exiles. Many a Seychellois gathered in the valley below to listen to the free concert. When the archbishop left Seychelles and returned to Cyprus, the house passed to an English businessman. On one occasion, the latter visited the archbishop and enquired about the large collection of bottles that he had found in the front garden of the Sans Souci house. The archbishop freely admitted that part of his agreement with the British Government over his exile was that he would receive a generous supply of his favourite wines. 'And now you know why we sang so well,' he added with a twinkle in his eye.

The ride up Sans Souci is unusual, through thick forest and heavy undergrowth, often scented by cinnamon, which opens up now and again to reveal stunning panoramas along the east coast. But be careful, particularly around bends, as there are no protective barriers on the sides of the road which, overhung by trees, is often slippery.

There is another FEBA transmission centre on the Sans Souci road, outside which a sign declares 'FEBA Radio — Christ to the World by Radio'. A little further along, there is a Forestry Division Sans Souci notice. Take the narrow road immediately after the signpost and drive up about 300 metres to a small car park where walk number five, 'Trois Frères', in the 'Nature Trail and Walks in Seychelles' series begins. This 2.2 kilometre walk — all uphill — leads through a section of the Morne Seychellois National Park to the summit of the highest of the 'Trois Frères' where the views over Mahé are stunning. The Morne Seychellois National Park, created in 1979, includes a large section of the central uplands of Mahé. Most of the island's fascinating plants and animals are given complete protection within its boundaries as part of a coordinated land management policy which includes commercial forestry and agriculture. Once at the summit, there are two possibilities for the descent — retracing your tracks, or continuing on to Le Niol.

Back on the Sans Souci road, there is a general store and a barrier, usually raised. For another excellent panorama of Victoria and much of the east coast, about 500 metres from the Forestry Division just after a sharp bend and before the walled garden of a house, turn left down a very rough track. Reaching a glacis, park your car and take the steps which lead to a viewing point high above Rochon Reservoir, where the vistas are breathtaking. This reservoir has a very large catchment area but a small capacity, so all excess water is piped to La Gogue Reservoir in the north, where the water catchment area is small but the capacity large.

As you rise even higher, through Sans Souci, the marked drop in temperature is noticeable. Number eight, 'Val Riche-Copolia', in the 'Nature Trails and Walks in Seychelles' series begins at a signboard on the side of the road. This shaded walk through the forest of the Morne Seychellois National Park leads up to a huge expanse of granite about 500 metres above sea level where there are spectacular views of the east coast. Approximately two hours are necessary to complete the whole walk. Almost at the crest of the road, two small cannons mark the entrance to the drive of the home of President Albert René's ex-wife.

Driving down the mountainside, the next point of interest is the ruins of the Capucin Mission. Originally this area was known as Venns Town and was established as a school for the children of the slaves liberated by the British Anti-Slavery patrol. While Arab dhows carried slaves up to the Red Sea, this patrol tried to end slave-trading on the East African coast by seizing the dhows and taking the freed slaves to Seychelles. At Venns Town, the children were given a basic education while their parents worked on the coastal plantations.

A magnificent avenue of sandragon trees leads to the present viewing lodge, where Queen Elizabeth once surveyed the stunning views of the west coast. So, too, did the botanical artist, Marianne North, who visited Venns Town when the school was still in existence. She noted in her 1883 diary: 'The situation of Venns Town is one of the most magnificent in the world, and the silence of the forest around was only broken by the children's happy voices. From that flat-topped, isolated hill, one saw a long stretch of wild mountain coast, and many islands, some 2,000 feet below, across which long-tailed boatswain-birds were always flying; behind it, the highest peak of Mahé frowned down on us, often inky-black under the storm-clouds.'

Continuing down La Route Forêt Noire (Sans Souci), the terraces of the tea plantation soon appear bordering the roadside. Tea was first planted commercially on Mahé in 1962 and now covers 45 hectares. The tea plants benefit from an excellent location — high altitude and a climate blessed with equal amounts of sunshine and rain which gives the tea a balanced bouquet.

There is one final walk, number six 'Tea Factory-Morne Blanc' in the 'Nature Trails and Walks in Seychelles' series, still to be completed on this road. The trail starts just above the tea plantation, on the right-hand side of the road. This relatively short walk through the shaded forest of the Morne Seychellois National Park leads to the summit of Morne Blanc where there are spectacular views of the west coast.

One hundred metres down the road, the Seychelles Tea Tavern is an excellent place to sit and enjoy a cup of tea and a cake, after either the long drive from Victoria or one of the hikes through the hills. It is also possible to visit the small factory below where 130 employees work to produce 40 tonnes of tea annually.

From now on, it's all downhill to Port Glaud, the small village which nestles at the bottom of La Route Forêt Noire (Sans Souci) and borders the coastline. Port Glaud has a health centre, school and, at the junction with the coast road, a police station.

Additional Information

National Archives & National Heritage
La Bastille
Pointe Conan, Mahé
Tel: 224-777
9am to 4pm Monday to Friday
9am to 12noon Saturday

Kreolfleurage Parfums
Northeast Point, Mahé
Tel: 241-329
9am to 5pm Monday to Friday
9am to 12noon Saturday

Vladimir Art Studio
Glacis, Mahé
Tel: 261-211
When he's at home, the studio is open

Ron Gerlach Batiks
Beau Vallon, Mahé
Tel: 266-670
10am to 12noon, 2pm to 5pm
Monday to Friday
10am to 12 noon Saturday

Antonio Filippin
The Yellow Gallery
Beau Vallon
Mahé
Tel: 247-658
10am to 5pm Monday to Saturday

Gordon Pottery
Le Niol
Mahé
9am to 6pm Monday to Saturday
2pm to 6pm Sunday

Tea Factory
Sans Souci
Mahé
Tel: 378-221 8am to 4pm Monday to Friday (preferably in the morning when there is more activity)

Tea Tavern
Sans Souci
Mahé
Tel: 378-221
9am to 5pm Monday to Friday
9am to 4pm Saturday

3
THE WEST COAST OF MAHÉ

In general, the west coast of Mahé from Port Launay in the north to Police Bay, the southernmost beach open to the public, is less populated than the east coast. Most of the interesting features on this side of the island are found in the natural beauty. Port Launay Marine National Park is famous for its excellent snorkeling and SCUBA diving grounds. The island of Thérèse is a beautiful, uninhabited island with an interesting history and 'pirate graves'. Grand Anse and Anse Intendance, many argue, are more picturesque and certainly less spoilt than Beau Vallon. The west coast is not just for nature lovers, however. There are several artists' studios — a sculptor, two painters and a cooperative pottery — to be visited in the area around Anse à la Mouche and Baie Lazare.

From the La Route Forêt Noire (Sans Souci) junction in Port Glaud, travel north-west along the coastal road, passing The Cradle of Love President's Village, which is an orphanage. The road is so close to the sea at this point that if the tide is high, pedestrians and cars are often covered by spray. Sand on the road is testament to this. Of interest, are the giant granite steps on Pointe l'Escalier, at the southern end of Port Launay. It is said that these steps were carved out by Polynesians centuries ago, but they may be a natural phenomenon. Out to sea, on the left, lies the uninhabited island of Thérèse, where pirates are thought to have sheltered once they had plundered ocean-going ships. Ancient graves on the top of the island are thought to belong to pirates. From the graves, there are excellent views across to Mahé.

There are excellent snorkeling sites off the northern coast of Thérèse, where there is a large lagoon. The island is reserved for the exclusive use of guests resident at three nearby hotels.

Back on Mahé, the coastal road rises and narrows as it leaves the village of Port Glaud. There are no road markings, so drive carefully. Houses on the hillside have excellent views across to Thérèse Island and closer inshore, L'Islette, one of the smallest granite islands in Seychelles. Directly opposite the island of L'Islette, there is a cross with 'Mission 1950' inscribed on its base. On the inland (right) side of the road, the general store run by a Mrs M Damay has been accommodated in the front room of the proprietor's house, and there is another general store from where big-game fishing, tours to nearby islands and snorkeling in the Port Launay Marine National Park are organised by Blue Bird Big Game and Bottom Fishing.

The Sundown Restaurant is located right next to the coast as the road dips down to sea level once more. As the name would indicate, the outside terrace is a great place to sit and enjoy an aperitif while watching the sun set. It is also an intimate place to taste Seychelles home-style cooking at its best, including mouth-watering curries and baked fish. Attached to The Sundown Restaurant is Celine's Boutique.

The 'boat-house' for L'Islette, where the free boat service to the island departs, is just after The Sundown. To call the ferry service into action, you may have to jump up and down, wave your arms wildly, toot your car horn or flash the car's headlights, un-til the attention of someone on the island is attracted. Wait patiently and, sooner or later, a boat will arrive. L'Islette offers both accommodation and a restaurant. The 12 bungalows for rent are particularly popular with honeymoon couples and those who come to Seychelles to marry. The restaurant specialises in seafood and Creole cuisine and is popular with locals as well as tourists, particularly on Sunday at lunchtime when a Creole bar-becue is served.

Almost opposite the boat-house is the small, simple Roman Catholic Church of Saints Pierre and Paul, which dates back to the late 19th century. Benches line the interior of the church which includes a small balcony above the entrance, reached by a flight of stairs to the right as you enter. Halfway up the stairs, is where the bell is rung to call the congregation to church. The only touches of extravagance in the church are three beautiful stained-glass windows behind the altar.

A small side road next to the church leads to the Port Glaud waterfall. It is better to walk than drive as there are few places to park en route. Mangrove swamps, the original vegetation of Mahé's lowlands, on the left-hand side of the road are where the famous Seychelles crocodile used to live. This type of vegetation made it very difficult for early settlers to land.

The road rises gently, passing a number of modern houses, with beautifully kept gardens. Chickens, meanwhile, squawk loudly as they run loose and pigs grunt from impossibly small sties. Above all this cacophony of sound, however, it is possible to hear the fast-flowing L'Islette River and the waterfall — especially if there has been heavy rain.

Close to the top of the road, which deteriorates into little more than a track, a barrier of sorts — two pieces of wood stuck into the ground with a piece of rope strung between them — marks the entrance to Waterfall Farm. The farm supplies hotels with seasonal produce, but its grounds are by no means extensive. From there on, labels indicate the names of most of the trees and plants — takamaka, avocado, coast apple and citronel for example. Continue up the driveway and ring the bell. One of the farm staff greets visitors, has them sign in the guest book and pay a small entrance fee.

Afterwards, visitors are taken to the waterfall, one of the largest in Seychelles, where it is possible to swim. Endemic plants such as the thief palm grow close to the pool into which the

waterfall cascades. If lucky, you may also catch sight of some other creatures unique to the islands, such as prawns.

Return to the main coast road by the same route. From the L'Islette boat-house, it is possible to drive about another three kilometres as far as Anse Souillac. This narrow road runs along the shores of the Port Launay Marine National Park, an enclosed sandy cove with a fringing reef. The deeper parts of the reef which fringe the rocky headlands are in particularly good condition and soft corals flourish. The main feature of this park, however, is the marked contrast between the shoreline, which is interspersed with sandy beaches and mangrove forests, and the steep, forested lower slopes of Morne Seychellois. Conception Island lies directly opposite the bay of Port Launay. It has no beach, so it is difficult to land there except in very calm conditions. Off its north-western shore, there is excellent diving and big game fishing in the area is usually very fruitful.

Beyond Anse Souillac, the extreme western tip of Mahé forms a sheltered bay which marks the boundary of the Baie Ternay Special Reserve. It is only possible to visit this area, which covers an area of 80 hectares, from the seaward side — most easily from Beau Vallon. The main features of the Special Reserve are the

The Mahé Beach Hotel was built to resemble a cruise liner from afar

Opposite: Most of the beaches are usually empty except at weekends when the locals use them

reef, which offers refuge to large numbers of fish, and the beach, which is a breeding ground for the hawksbill turtle.

It is not possible to progress past Anse Souillac by car, because the road meets the gates of the Baie Ternay National Youth Service (NYS) camp. The NYS, two years of compulsory education in practical, cultural, political and social activities for 15-year-olds, was introduced by René's government. However, it proved unpopular and, following a series of public demonstrations, the NYS was later made voluntary, reduced to one year, and its provisions modified. At the NYS gates, it is necessary to retrace one's tracks to Port Glaud.

Returning south through Port Glaud, just after the turning to Sans Souci, there is a well-stocked general store run by a Mrs J Bibi. Continue along the coast road, passing the tiny island of Petite Ile, which is not really an island as it is joined to the mainland by a jumble of granite rocks. Around the corner, built like the superstructure of a cruise ship and much more visible than any other seaside hotel in Seychelles, is the Mahé Beach Hotel which, until 1992, was the Sheraton. This is the one hotel on the island to have sidestepped the law that no hotel should be built higher than the surrounding palm trees.

An elegant feature of the hotel is the 20 acres of tropical gardens. These gardens run down to a sheltered sandy cove, created by a spit of granite boulders, where it is safe to swim year-round. The hotel also has use of Thérèse, where many additional watersports, including windsurfing, canoeing and snorkeling, are on offer. Sea scooters, water-skiing, glass-bottom boat tours, big-game fishing with one of the island's most famous fishers, Gonsalves Larue, known to one and all as 'Speedy', and SCUBA diving are offered at extra cost. Boat transfers to the island leave in the morning, either from the hotel grounds or Port Glaud depending on the weather, and return in the afternoon.

The hotel has 172 rooms, three restaurants — Au Jardin is set in the tropical gardens — serving a variety of international and Creole cuisine, several bars and the Cococabana disco, which opens on Thursdays, Fridays and Saturdays. A tennis court, badminton court, air-conditioned squash court, volleyball court, table football and other indoor games are also on offer. Guided daily outings from the hotel take guests to the Port Glaud waterfall, around the hotel's gardens to identify all the tropical plants, and to Thérèse Island to follow the pirate trail.

From the entrance to the hotel, the road bears away from the coast and climbs steadily into the district of Beolière. The houses there are tucked well away, behind a blanket of rich vegetation that includes jackfruit and breadfruit trees, albizias — easily recognisable by their flat tops — which often have vanilla growing up their trunks, and a host of other tropical trees. Over the brow of the hill, the beautiful bay of Grand Anse may be glimpsed in the distance, through the trees.

Coming down the hill, you pass the Hill Store, a modern general store, where phonecards are on sale, and a signpost for the Patchouli Curio Shop, which no longer exists. The flagged entrance to the Equator Hotel is on the right. A beautifully landscaped drive leads down to the hotel, which clings to a large granite escarpment that slopes down into the sea. The design of the swimming-pool makes excellent use of this escarpment, as the water has been channelled to cascade down the massive granite rocks into the pool. Unfortunately, the small beach at the foot of the cliffs only appears between September and May. Other sporting activities include tennis, volleyball, aerobics and the watersports facilities of Thérèse Island. There is also a regular programme of events such as fun runs and organised walks. Accommodation is provided in 56 suites — each with lounge, bathroom and wide verandah facing the sea. The hotel also boasts a conference room. There are two restaurants — La Palafitte with spectacular, uninterrupted views across the bay to Île Aux Vaches, and the coffee shop which, together with the Takamaka Bar, is situated in the centre of the swimming-pool. This is the best venue in which to watch 'Sokwe' — one of the few groups of musicians and dancers which still perform traditional songs and dances. The group visits the hotel once a week to put on its show.

Continuing along the main road, pass the Beolière Health Centre and, just before reaching level ground once more, there is a turning for the Ministry of Agriculture and Fisheries Crop Development Division Research Station Grand Anse. The modern Grand Anse Supermarket is on the opposite side of the road.

The public housing development as you enter the village of Grand Anse, is where many of the workers from the government's research stations are housed. Grand Anse beach can be glimpsed through the takamaka trees on the opposite side of the road. Grand Anse itself, a huge sweep of white coral sand, may be beautiful and deserted, but it is also dangerous. The beach is very rarely safe for swimming, because there are strong currents and a powerful undertow, particularly from May to October (during the south-easterly monsoon), when huge waves pummel

Waterskier speeds over the calm waters of the Indian Ocean

into shore. One British colonial governor ignored the danger signs and drowned.

Right at the entrance to the beach a sharp left-hand bend takes the road away from the coast. On the right is Grand Anse School, with its huge red-earth playground. The rich coastal plain here has given rise to experimental plots on either side of this road, which under the control of the Ministry of Agriculture and Fisheries Crop Development Research Station, have been planted with many different varieties of tropical fruit. At one stage, the success of this research station in identifying high-yield bean and cabbage strains back-fired — over-production meant the market became flooded with these commodities.

There is a timber yard just before the left-hand turn for La Misère, which is the mountain road most frequently used to cross over to the east coast — for several reasons. It is shorter and less tortuous than the Sans Souci road and, particularly at night, it is much safer to travel via La Misère, which is much more densely populated than the other cross-hill routes and where you are more likely to find help, should your car break down. Opposite the turn, several large aerials mark the location of the BBC Indian Ocean Relay Station. This short wave relay sta-

Crystal-clear waters surround Thérèse Island

tion was established in 1989 to broadcast to East and Southern Africa and is the biggest consumer of electricity on the island.

The Catholic church of La Sainte Famille in Grand Anse is very simple and houses a rather dusty confession box. Opposite the church is a card call box and a general store which is one of the few in this area to open on Sundays. Another general store just around the corner is run by a member of the Dangkow family.

Nearby Le Meridien Barbarons, the second Meridien hotel in Seychelles, opened in 1978. The 123-room hotel is set in a tropical garden that harmonises perfectly with its surroundings. Built on a beautiful white sandy beach which is perfect for snorkeling, but not so good for swimming. The hotel has several restaurants, all with an excellent reputation for producing good food, be it international or local cuisine. The hotel provides facilities, free of charge for guests, for tennis, mini golf, snorkeling, volleyball, water polo, swimming and indoor games.

The watersports centre on Thérèse Island, off Port Glaud, is also open to guests of Le Meridien Barbarons. The hotel organises big-game fishing trips and SCUBA diving outings at additional cost. Evening entertainment is provided by local bands, *sega* groups and cabaret performers, while there is free transportation to the casino at The Plantation Club Hotel. The lobby at Le Meridien Barbarons is one of two locations (the other is the Reef Golf Club Hotel on the east coast of Mahé) where bicycles, both touring and mountain styles, may be hired from Hercules Bicycle Hire. Cycling is a healthy and environmentally friendly way to tour the island and Hercules organises excursions to various places of interest in the south of the island. Hercules also delivers to other parts of the island. Ring 373 039 for more details.

Back on the main road is another SMB concern, Indian Ocean Nurseries, which grows orchids for export. The whole area, to the right and to the left, as far as the base of the mountains, used to belong to a family by the name of Troian and was known as the Barbarons Estate. The remains of the coconut plantation are still evident today. Close to the beach, an old two-storey building is a deserted cinnamon oil distillery. The low-lying houses a little further along the road were built for the plantation workers, but are now all privately owned.

On the right-hand side of the road is the start of the driveway to Chateau D'Eau, the colonial plantation house which has been converted to a Relais des Îles. Still under the control of the Troian family, this beautiful guesthouse offers French and Creole cuisine, as well as windsurfing and horse-riding facilities.

The coastal road then climbs and falls into the village of Anse Boileau where the reef is close to the shore, and there is a lot of coral coverage under shallow water. It is not good for swimming because of the coral and the silt, which tends to flood into the bay from several rivers, particularly after a heavy rainfall. However, Anse Boileau is picturesque. Granite rocks rise out of the water and takamaka trees fringe the back of the beach, just in front of the road. It is also of historical importance, according to research carried out by island historians, which indicates that Anse Boileau is more likely than Baie Lazare to be the bay into which Lazare Picault sailed on his first voyage of exploration for the French in 1742.

The first building driving south through the village of Anse Boileau is a general store. Soon after this, to the left of the road, are the Anse Boileau Health Centre and the Auberge Anse Boileau, where the restaurant Chez Plume is located. Chez Plume, which receives excellent reviews, serves a mix of international and Creole cuisines, and specialises in seafood. Its crab in ginger is particularly popular with regulars.

There are several more general stores in the village before the road starts to rise. At the top of a small knoll is a shrine and further along the road is a football pitch. In between the two is a turning to the Montagne Posee Road, a narrow, twisting road that leads to Anse Aux Pins on the east coast. If you follow this road until Bon Espoir, a small paved road at the crest of the hill leads towards the Cable and Wireless station where the satellite dish used for international communications has been erected. It is also the centre for radio communications with ships and the outer islands of Seychelles. You may contact the Bon Espoir station by phoning 375 733 if you are planning a private trip to one of the outer islands. The helpful staff will willingly provide information on weather conditions and pass messages on to the islands to inform them of the expected arrival of visitors.

A small parking area at the beginning of this paved road marks the start of trail number seven, 'La Reserve-Brulee' in the 'Nature Trails and Walks in Seychelles' series. Along this walk is the best area of palm forest remaining on Mahé — five of the six palms (the *coco-de-mer* is absent, of course) unique to Seychelles are to be seen, together with numerous other endemic plants and animals. The trail also affords excellent views of the west coast.

Continuing along the west coast road, past Anse Boileau Police Station and a branch of Barclays Bank there is a turning, just before Anse Boileau School, to Our Lady of Seven Sorrows Roman Catholic church, otherwise known as 'Notre Dame des Sept Doleurs'. One of the more attractive churches on the island, it has a beautiful wooden ceiling, nicely carved interior roof supports and simple wooden benches. There are many stained glass windows on both sides of the church and an ornate altar. White, pink and pale blue are the dominant colours of the decor.

Farther along the coast road, Anse Boileau District Council and Community Centre is on the right-hand side, next door to a children's playground. There is another general store, at which point the road leads inland. Follow the main road, as any secondary roads leading off this main road merely lead to residential districts of no particular interest to tourists.

An impressive white entrance marks the driveway to the Tec Tec Hotel and Restaurant, which was opened at the end of 1993. The drive to the hotel leads through the courtyards of several small houses, up a steep bank to the hotel itself. The six executive chalets all have views over Anse Louis, a quiet little cove which is easily accessible from the chalets. The restaurant, also open to non-residents, offers a choice of Creole and international dishes.

There is a dramatic view of a black and orange rock face opposite the entrance to the Tec Tec. After passing over Rivière du

Golden sunset over Anse à la Mouche

Rempart which leads into the sea at Anse Louis, a large boulder perches precariously atop another. Out to the right, there are stunning views along the west coast of Mahé which take in the offshore islands to the north-west.

Soon after, the road bends to reveal a sweeping vista of Anse à la Mouche, like Anse Boileau, a shallow, wide bay. From this slightly elevated position, it is possible to see the coral under the water reflecting different hues of green and blue, as well as black, which contrast sharply with the white breakers that crash over the reef and rocks. Anse à la Mouche is one of the calmest bays in Seychelles and ideal for swimming, although at low tide it may be necessary to walk out some distance. Alternatively, when the sea is calm and the sky clear, try lounging in the shallow water — it's almost like taking a hot bath. And don't worry, Anse à la Mouche is so named, not because it is swamped by flies (mouche in French), but because a ship called *La Mouche* was wrecked there in 1812. A cannon from the ship is on display at La Bastille at Pointe Conan.

Driving south into the village of Anse à la Mouche, the Oscar

au Capitaine Rouge restaurant (also known simply as Oscar's), which has a distinctly French atmosphere, is on the right-hand side. The fish soup, red snapper fillet in a passionfruit sauce, fillet steak in a tangy mustard sauce and fresh prawns sautéd in garlic and fresh herbs all come highly recommended. Built out over the water, the restaurant also has great sea views. The village has two general stores before the turn into Les Cannelles which leads through a coconut plantation before it twists and turns uphill. The first turning on the right leads to the home of the honorary Swiss Consul and the home-cum-studio of Tom Bowers, a sculptor.

Born of gypsy origin in London in 1936, Tom finished his education at South-West Essex School of Art, where he studied sculpture and graphics, and at Guildford Photographic School. His first job was in advertising, where he worked for major agencies, such as J. Walter Thompson and Saatchi and Saatchi as a photographer. He used many unusual props, many of them unavailable commercially and so he had to make them himself. The work led him back to sculpture.

When he visited Seychelles in 1981 he fell in love with the islands and returned many times before he and his family decided to make the country their home in 1986. The island landscapes, as well as the charm, style and grace of the local people, are his inspiration. Typical works include a musician with his drum and a man strolling home with a string of fish. He sculpts in a real 20th-century material, a resin originally developed to repair space and military vehicles. It can be moulded and shaped, but coated with a hardening agent it becomes rock solid. The finished material bears an uncanny resemblance to the local granite. The sculptures are sent to South Africa and cast in bronze in limited editions of around ten. Prices start from about SR3,500.

As you carry on east along Les Canelles, you reach the peak of a hill and then travel downhill, to the Benitier souvenir shop on the left-hand side of the road. It stocks a lot of clothing and accepts several credit cards. It is opposite a small, typical Seychellois house. Further down the hill, a turning opposite a general store leads to the Ministry of Health Psychiatric Hospital. Before the 1930s, the mentally ill were sent to Mauritius, which sent its lepers to Seychelles. The first psychiatric hospital was founded in Anse Royale, and finally found its resting place here.

Descending the hill, the corrugated iron roofs of several modern houses are visible from the road. The road reaches level ground by a general store located at the junction with a secondary road known as Sweet Escott Road. Les Canelles then continues on, through shady groves, the remains of a coconut plantation and some more modern agricultural activities to the east coast road. The Anse Royale Community Centre is situated to the left of this junction.

Back on the west coast, the road south through Anse à la Mouche passes several beach houses and the self-catering Blue Lagoon Chalets. There are four chalets, each divided into two, with a total of eight rooms and 16 beds. Each chalet has a kitchenette, sitting room and wide verandah. The whole establishment is well-maintained and the rooms spotlessly clean. As a result, it is very popular and maintains a high occupancy rate. The Anchor Cafe and Pizzeria, where there is a coin-operated phone box is next door. The cafe is superb for reasonably priced fish and chips, pizzas or local curries.

Leaving Anse à la Mouche bay, La Residence Villas-Apartments stand at the top of a short, steep drive with an excellent view over the sea. The three chalets and three apartments may be rented on either a short-term or long-term basis.

Anse aux Poules Bleues, the small beach just after Anse à la

Mouche, is backed by the remains of an old coconut plantation. There is a Creole restaurant called La Sirène at the most southern end of the beach. It has a good, shady location overlooking the sea and there is often a refreshing sea breeze in which to relax during the heat of the day. Specialities include fruit bat (when available), octopus salad and, for dessert, different flavoured ice-creams laced with alcohol.

Around the corner close to La Sirène is another general store. At this point, the road heads inland and passes a wooden planta-tion house, the home and studio of Seychelles' most famous resident painter, Michael Adams. Michael, who is British, arrived in Seychelles in 1972 from Uganda 'to escape Idi Amin who was chopping up my friends'. His initial interest in the islands was prompted by a conversation with a friend who had told him that it was a fantastic place where 'all the men wear hats, and they never take them off, even when they go to bed'. He came to ex-perience this magical place for himself for a short period of rest and recreation, but he never left. Somewhat surprisingly, the in-spiration for his paintings comes not from the sea, by which he is surrounded, but from the island's interiors. 'I'm a jungle person,' he says. An early childhood spent in Malaysia, where his father was a rubber planter, goes some way to explaining this.

Michael is fascinated by the complexity of the land's interior and the way everything in nature tries to be organised but fails. 'If you look at a bunch of leaves coming off a branch, they are all trying to be exactly the same,' he explains, 'but they are always failing and it's that failure which I like to capture in my paint-ings. Chaos is absolutely essential to me — a domestic garden does not provide the same inspiration.'

Most of his paintings, to date, have depicted the greenery and growth of local spots, such as the Botanical Gardens and Praslin's Vallée de Mai. There are other subjects, however, such as the Northolme Hotel (hidden behind a mass of foliage), a rare sea scene, a few of domestic Seychelles life and the odd street scene. In future, Michael says, he is going to move away from jungles to work with 'people in landscape', concentrating first on bus stops. His paintings are not without humour and, in one of the street scenes Michael has painted, a local Seychellois walks one way, while his head faces the other — summing up the magical and mystical aura that pervades the islands.

He paints the basic structure of a picture directly from his source of inspiration and then returns to his studio to 'decorate madly' and build up the 'tapestry'. The resulting paintings are a

Tom Bowers sculpts in a resin originally developed to repair space and military vehicles

blast of colour and intricate details, which take at least a full month's work to complete. The silk-screen prints that are meticulously reproduced by hand from his paintings — in editions of up to 500 — often take longer to finish as up to 120 different colours may have to be applied. The prints are popular souvenirs.

Leaving Michael's studio, turn right continuing in a southerly direction, past one or two typical Seychellois houses and a general store, to enter the village of Baie Lazare. Opposite a general store, Chemin Anse Soleil, a rough road (no more than two concrete strips at its best) leads to the three small beaches of Anse Gouvernement, Anse La Liberté (also known as Petite Anse) and Anse Soleil. Roughly a kilometre from the junction, there is a shrine by the side of the track. After another kilometre, the road divides. Carry straight on for about one-and-a-half kilometres to reach Anse Gouvernement or turn to the right and continue along the track for about one kilometre to reach Anse Soleil, a small, beautifully secluded cove.

 In Baie Lazare, a little further up the hill from the junction of Chemin Anse Soleil, a signpost marks the Val d'Endor Pottery.

Vladimir Tarakanoff uses the verdant landscape and sunny environment as his sources of inspiration

Follow the road (sometimes little more than a rough track which is bumpy at the best of times), called Chemin Dame Le Roi, for almost three kilometres through pineapple plantations and past the odd house, until you reach the pottery. Opened in 1988, this pottery has its own clay unit operated by two employees where black, red, white and yellow clays are dug from local earth. The clay is worked by four potters into mugs, vases, bowls and trinkets which are sold to both tourists and ordered — often *en masse* — by local clients such as hotels.

The pottery's speciality is hand building, rather than wheel-based work. The glazes are also produced locally — the ashes of dry leaves from coconut trees and cinnamon plants are mixed with an oxide to produce colours unique to Seychelles. Creations include cute tortoises with egg cups on their backs and vases in the shape of fish, the tails of which form the shape of a vase. Prices range between SR20 for a small tortoise and SR300 for a large vase. Val d'Endor Pottery also sells pieces at The Plantation Club Hotel and CODEVAR in Victoria's Camion Hall.

Back in Baie Lazare, another signpost just past the police station points to the studio of artist Donald Adelaide. Follow the track and the studio is about 100 metres from the main road. Donald, who was born in 1957, is predominantly self-taught. However, he has had lessons from Michael Adams, and this is evident in his work, which is similar. His naive water-colours are dominated by landscapes and scenes of village life in Baie Lazare. Very rarely does he work in oils. The inspiration for his work comes from what is around him, but also from the music of his idols who include Michael Jackson, Guns'n'Roses and Dire Straits. He usually sketches directly from life, but then returns to his studio to fill in the bright colours which are his trademark. Donald sells both prints and originals. Prices for prints start at SR100, while those for originals are at around SR2,000. The only outlets, other than his studio, from which he sells, are Le Meridien Barbarons and Christy's Art Gallery in town.

Next door to the petrol station in the centre of Baie Lazare, there is a general store and the Baie Lazare Community Centre, which has a children's playground and a basketball court, and opposite it is a cemetery. The school close to the graveyard is attached to the village church dedicated to St Francis of Assisi. A massive mock-Gothic stone edifice, built on the top of a small hill, it has a lofty belltower which is worth climbing, despite the state of the spiral staircase, because the view of the bay below is breathtaking. There is no stained glass in the church, but there are some stunning biblical murals on all three sides of the altar. Otherwise it is very simple, with slatted windows and a gallery at the back of the church. Outside the church, a round monument marks the centenary anniversary of the parish of Baie Lazare, inaugurated on 3 July 1888.

Pass through the village of Baie Lazare and the entrance to the Plantation Club Hotel and Casino is on the right. The reason for the hotel's name is obvious as you drive from the main road up to the central complex. The whole property is built among the remains of an old coconut plantation. A small building to the right of the driveway, often adorned with palm fronds and tropical flowers, is used for weddings. To the left of the driveway is a modern building, constructed in colonial style which will eventually house the casino, a conference room and another restaurant.

A sprawling hotel, The Plantation Club Hotel is the biggest on the island, offering around 200 large, split-level rooms. An interesting feature of the hotel's lobby is the large ceramic mural at the back of a rock garden, which comes complete with moving water. The mural — a reproduction of Michael Adams' painting of the waterfall on Praslin — was created in Thailand from 1,300 ceramic tiles. Once they arrived in Seychelles, the tiles took two whole days to reassemble.

Facilities at The Plantation Club Hotel include several bars and restaurants such as the sophisticated Lazare's Speciality Restaurant, swimming-pool, SCUBA dive centre, snorkeling equipment, windsurfers, pedaloes, canoes, row boats, health centre, tennis courts, volleyball court, badminton court, shuffle-board court, petanque court and children's playground. The hotel fronts on to Baie Lazare beach, which is not ideal for swimming, but provides excellent snorkeling opportunities. The Planters' Casino and the Helicopter Seychelles helispot, within the extensive grounds and from which scenic tours of Mahé are conducted, are added attractions.

From the hotel's main entrance the coast road leads into the hamlet of Anse Gaulettes, which has several general stores and the Anse Gaulettes Bar and Restaurant offering Chinese and Creole food. Close to the beach, an old anchor, on a stone pedestal bears the following words: 'This monument was erected with the help of the French Government and inaugurated by Mrs Sylvette Frichot, Minister of Local Government, Culture and Sports, commemorating the two hundred and fiftieth anniversary of the arrival of Captain Lazare Picault on 21 November 1742 in the first expedition to the Seychelles.' Ironically, this is now thought not to be the bay into which Picault sailed. That honour is reserved for Anse Boileau.

Opposite Baie Lazare beach, which is backed by takamaka trees, is the Benitier Beach Boutique (a sister shop to the boutique on Chemin Les Cannelles). It sells traditional hats, shells, boxes, model pirogues, spices, teas, locally made suntan oil, shorts, T-shirts and pareos. From the boutique, the road climbs to a bend, where the entrance to the Lazare Picault chalets — nine thatched rondavels offering a total of 14 rooms well-positioned to overlook the bay — is located. The guesthouse offers snorkeling, windsurfing and fishing.

The road takes on dramatic dimensions at Pointe Maravi, where it has been built into the cliff face, creating a jagged left road edge. On the right-hand side, a host of casuarina trees and rocks tumble down into the sea. Look out for the bright pink fruit of the wild pineapple along this stretch of road.

The next bay along the west coast, Anse Takamaka, is so called — not surprisingly — because a profusion of takamaka trees

fringes it. It is ideal for snorkeling, but swimmers should note the sign warning of dangerous offshore currents, particularly during the south-east monsoon (between May and October). The Chez Baptista restaurant at the southern end of Takamaka Beach is particularly popular with Italian tourists. To reach it, either park close to the main road and walk along the beach or take a small sand road at the back of the beach to a wooden bridge which crosses over a mangrove swamp area. Park there and walk across the bridge to the restaurant.

Chez Baptista is in a particularly picturesque area where pirogues are pulled up on to the beach into their shelters, papaya, banana and coconut trees grow freely in the background, and the beach is no more than a step away. So close, in fact, that the sea almost laps at the customers' feet during high tide. Chez Baptista, described as a 'rustique restaurant', has a low thatch roof, sand floor, bench seating and tables, and typical local decor, such as fish traps, known as 'casier', and stuffed turtles on the walls. The menu — in a variety of languages — includes avocado, octopus and palm heart salad, fresh fish and sirloin steak, and a number of desserts, such as fresh fruit or ice-cream.

Meanwhile the main road heads inland, through an over-

Helicopter Seychelles offers regular scenic flights over Mahé as well as transfers to other islands

grown coconut plantation, passing some modern houses, before it starts to climb, passing more modern houses and a general store run by Lewis Samson. This marks the start of the village of Quatre Bornes which has several more general stores. In between the buildings of Takamaka School, a sharp, steep turn leads to the stone-built Roman Catholic Church of St Mary Magdalene. Of simple design, with a corrugated iron roof, the church has an impressive mural behind the altar, a shrine to its right and the pulpit on the left. Small paintings line both walls and at the front there is some abstract, seemingly Mondrian-inspired, stained glass. The Takamaka Health Centre and the Quatre Bornes Police Station are also in the village.

The signpost to Intendance, which indicates that this well-known beach is only two kilometres away, is opposite a coin-operated call box. The concrete road that leads down to Anse Intendance passes the Intendance Shop which sells souvenirs, ice-cream, beer, soft drinks, snacks, cold wine, sandwiches and hamburgers, as well as T-shirts, *coco-de-mer*, complete shells, jewellery made from turtleshell (the proprietor said it was the last they would sell) and various coconut shell items, which local crafts people now use as an alternative.

Instead of taking a right-hand turn to Intendance it is possible to continue along Grande Police road for two or three kilometres, to Anse Corail and Anse Bazarca. It is not possible to reach Police Bay. Before this point you come face-to-face with a sign that warns there is no entry because the area is a military zone, out of bounds to the public. There is little else of interest along this road — the roadsides are covered with clumps of bamboo, banana and coconut trees — but it is wild and sparsely inhabited.

Anse Intendance, however, is one of the most beautiful beaches in Seychelles. Remote and tranquil, with incredibly soft sand, Intendance is often deserted. Several people have drowned there. One interesting oddity at Anse Intendance is that among the hundreds of coconuts that back on to the beach, one has two separate crowns emerging from its trunk. Kanti, the retailer and local historian in Victoria, believes bad spirits inhabit Intendance. He tells a tale of how, when film star Peter Sellers was thinking of building a hotel there, he asked Kanti to come up with a name. Kanti asked his spiritual friends for an auspicious name. Since none were proffered Sellers took it as a sign that no hotel built in that location would prosper. There is now a restaurant, La Jolie Rose, which serves Creole food.

Additional Information

Tom Bowers
Chemin Les Canelles
Mahé
Tel: 371 518
Every day, preferably during daylight hours

Michael Adams
Anse aux Poules Bleues
Mahé
Tel: 361 006
9am to 4pm Monday to Friday
9am to 12 noon Saturday
(Phone ahead if in doubt to make appointment outside of these hours.)

Val d'Endor Pottery
Val d'Endor
Mahé
Tel: 371 358
8am to 4pm Monday to Friday

Donald Adelaide
Baie Lazare
Mahé
No telephone
9am to 6pm every day

Planters Casino
The Plantation Club Hotel
Baie Lazare
Mahé
Tel: 371 588
8pm to 2am every day

4
THE EAST COAST OF MAHÉ

From the wild, scarcely habited areas in the south of the is-land, the face of the east coast changes dramatically the closer the road draws to Victoria. There is little to see at the start of this journey along the east coast, except unadulterated beauty and typical life in the Seychelles countryside. A little further north from Anse Royale, there is great snorkeling to be enjoyed around Île Souris and Pointe au Sel, known as Fairyland.

If you are interested in doing all the sights, life really starts to liven up around the area of Le Cap. La Marine (a model boat workshop), the Craft Village, a museum dedicated to the coconut and the Creole Institute are all in close proximity. Not too far ahead, there is also a nine-hole golf course, should you fancy a round.

Once past the airport, the coastline really builds up. The road passes first through the village of Cascade, noted for its waterfall and its church, then through an industrial zone where a whole host of factories including Seybrew are located. Already, the sub-urbs of Victoria are near. In Les Mamelles, there are two studios, conveniently located opposite each other, which are worth visit-ing. One belongs to painter Gerard Devoud, the other is the Seychelles Pottery Cooperative. After Les Mamelles, the choice is yours. Either take La Misère Road which leads back to Grand Anse on the west coast and passes the entrances to the United States Tracking station on the island en route, or carry on into the centre of Victoria.

From the deep south of the island, in the village of Quatre Bornes, the road wends its way down the hill for about one kilo-metre towards the east coast of Mahé. On reaching level ground, the road meanders through a coconut plantation until it reaches the coast and becomes the South Coast Road. Where the hill road meets the coast, a twelve-room guesthouse was opened in 1994.

The general store, no more than 100 metres along the South Coast Road in the direction of Victoria, is run by Walter Desaubin. The Allamanda Hotel Bar & Restaurant is opposite, housed in a modern, white-washed building built in grand, colonial style. Beautifully decorated inside, the 10-room hotel benefits from its quiet, secluded location on the picturesque Anse Forbans beach where it is safe to swim. Anse Forbans translates into English as Pirate's Cove, but there is no obvious gap in the offshore reef, so it seems unlikely this area was used by pirates. Facilities include a restaurant which serves both international and Creole cuisines, a piano bar and lounge, and a beach bar looking out to sea which also serves light meals.

The south-east of the island is mainly rural with a sprinkling of simple, modern houses and some areas under cultivation as banana and coconut plantations. From elevated positions along the road, there are excellent views to the north, along the east coast. Crashing waves create white breakers which contrast prettily with the many green and blue hues of the sea.

A couple of general stores are passed before reaching the fam-

Picturesque Allamanda Hotel is situated on the south-east coast of Mahé

ily-run Residence Bougainville, an old, traditional seven-roomed plantation house, set in tropical gardens overlooking the secluded beach of Anse Baleine. From its elevated position at the top of a steep drive from the coast road, the guesthouse provides excellent views out to sea. The restaurant specialises in Creole cuisine, and there is a bar, as well as opportunities for sailing and fishing.

A little further north along the South Coast Road a football pitch marks the Sisters of St Joseph of Cluny School, which is opposite the beige and brown Roman Catholic Church of St Joseph, from which it takes its name. This pretty church backs on to the sea. The arched supports inside are also painted beige and brown. The pews are simple, but there is some stained-glass and 14 paintings which depict Christ on the Way of the Cross have been mounted on either side of the church. The ornately carved wooden altar is painted gold and there are shrines and pulpits on both sides of it. The church also has an upstairs gallery. The outside statue of Christ with a small child carrying some flowers was presented by the Meghjee family.

Next door to the school on the other side of the road, is Sweet Escott Road, along which lies a small, peaceful cemetery. The far

Coconut plantation on Mahé

end of Sweet Escott Road meets the mountain pass road of Les Cannelles Road beside a general store run by Roch Richard 'Low. Take a right turn to re-join the South Coast Road. From the Church of St Joseph, the South Coast Road passes a general store, with a coin-operated phone box, and a traditional Creole house, then climbs over a small knoll and once more is amid coconut plantations. The Ministry of Agriculture and Fisheries, Livestock Division, Cattle Multiplication Unit, Anse Royale is on the left.

The village of Anse Royale starts where Les Cannelles Road meets the South Coast Road. The Holy Saviour's Anglican Church, one of the oldest on the island, is opposite the road junction. The church replaced a wooden chapel that originally stood at Pointe au Sel, just north of Anse Royale. The land for the church was donated by Jean-Baptiste Jumeau whose family also owned the building that now houses the Lenstiti Kreol which is further north along the South Coast Road. Construction of the church began in February 1889. It was built in a simple Gothic style with coral bricks and consecrated on 7 September 1893 by Bishop William Walsh. A bell calls worshippers to prayer and a plaque on the outside wall close to the road commemorates those who fell during the Great War. The inscription reads 'To the glory of God and in sacred memory of the undermentioned men of south Mahé that lost their lives in East Africa and France during the Great War 1914–1918' and is followed by 66 names. Above the main door, and the east and west windows, carved symbols depict sun, moon and stars. A small primary school stands next door to the church. From the back of the church, there is a stunning view of the narrow, three-kilometre-long Anse Royale beach. Soft sand and a protective coral reef make the beach a good place to laze and enjoy a little offshore snorkeling.

Anse Royale is so named because the area was settled in 1772 by an agent of the French king and is where the French set up a spice garden, known as 'Jardin du Roi' (the King's Garden). Several types of spice still grow wild on the hillside. In the village itself, there is a store and then, between the impressive building of the Polytechnic and the Anse Royale Health Clinic, a turning into Mon Plaisir Road. The Polytechnic offers a wide range of academic, technical and vocational courses for post-secondary and NYS students, including courses which lead to external qualifications.

Mon Plaisir Road marks the start of route number nine 'Anse Royale-Anse à la Mouche' in the 'Nature Trails and Walks in

Seychelles' series. The trail which is about five kilometres long, may take as long as four hours to complete. The first part of the road is through a wide flat coastal plain, which has always been in demand for agricultural purposes. In the 19th century, for example, much of the plain was planted with coconut trees for the production of copra.

Aromes de l'Ocean Indien, a joint venture between the Seychelles Government and French investors which opened in 1991, produces coconut cream for both local and export markets. Coconut cream is a natural product with no added preservatives that can be used in a variety of ways: for ice cream, coconut sorbet, flavouring for curries, stews, cream soups and cocktails. In full production, the factory requires 100,000 coconuts a month to produce 20 tons of coconut cream. Next to the factory is a distillery which was used only briefly for the distillation of cinnamon leaves to produce oil.

To the left of the trail, just before Durai's general store a path and some steps lead down to a small cemetery which has some interesting graves. Among them is that of the Irishman Dr J T Bradley, who arrived in Seychelles in 1901 and lived there until his death in 1942. A fascinating character, he eventually became the islands' Chief Medical Officer, as well as a member of both the Legislative and Executive Councils. After he retired in 1933, he set up the Clarion Press to publish a newspaper and also wrote the first concise *History of Seychelles*. It was to his daughter Dolly (by Mrs de Silva) and Dolly's husband, that the old plantation house in the Craft Village (further north on the South Coast Road) was given as a wedding present.

From Durai's, Mon Plaisir Road rises steeply to a large concrete cross, erected in 1985 by the Roman Catholic Church. Further ahead, a tiny general store is tagged on to the side of a house, and at the middle of a hairpin bend, stands a Roman Catholic Chapel, built in the 1980s from donated materials, hence its old appearance. The chapel is distinguished from other corrugated iron buildings by the cross above the front door. The road continues just a few hundred kilometres more up the hill, before petering out into a dirt track, along which it is possible to walk, but not drive, to Anse à la Mouche.

Return to Anse Royale, where the village police station is opposite the start of Mon Plaisir Road. There is also a branch of Banque Francaise Commerciale, several general stores and a petrol station, opposite which is the Kaz Creole restaurant, serving a combination of Creole and continental dishes, where you may eat either outside, under the trees, with the sand under your feet, or in the old colonial-style house. The restaurant also has its own watersports centre.

At the north end of the village stands a typical plantation house and further on, a tarred side road. Park there if you wish to enjoy some of Seychelles' underwater sights. From the northern end of Anse Royale, there are excellent snorkeling sites close to the small offshore island of Ile Souris and a little further along at Pointe au Sel, known locally as Fairyland. Île Souris is easily recognisable — a small, palm tree covered rocky outcrop — as the archetypal tropical island.

Beyond Anse Royale, the road rises to give impressive views north along the east coast. A small hamlet accommodates Lai Ti's general store before the road dips to sea level, right next to the water. On this long, fairly straight stretch is La Marine, Atelier Maquette de Bateaux, where scale models of historic sailing ships are meticulously copied from detailed plans obtained from the Naval Museum in Paris. The craft of creating exact replicas of old ships was introduced to Seychelles in 1979 and the islands' model boat makers have established an international reputation for quality and attention to detail. It is painstaking work, requiring a great deal of concentration and many man hours. For example, it takes at least 180 working hours to reproduce a model of *La Marie-Jeanne*, a Breton coastal sailing boat of 1908. The more expensive models, which may take up to 1,000 man hours to produce, have decks made of teak and metal fittings of copper and bronze. It is possible to watch craftsmen at work, each one producing a particular feature of the boat. The finished models are on sale in the showroom next door, which also sells wooden key rings, basic wooden toys and original watercolours. Prices for the boats range between SR1,200 and SR20,000. An old white plantation house next to La Marine is under government control.

Ty-Foo restaurant at Le Cap offers reasonable Creole and Chinese cuisine in a simple setting. The fried octopus, sweet and sour pork and fish curries are all recommended. The Sadeco administration pig farm is just past Ty-Foo.

The road once again borders a coconut plantation, in the middle of which is the old plantation house, now the central focus of the Craft Village. The 1870 plantation house was built in the middle of a large property known as the St Roch Estate, which stretched from the coast to the top of the mountain. In 1926, a Mrs de Silva bought the estate and presented it to her daughter,

The Craft Village on Mahé houses traditional examples of architecture along with a Creole speciality restaurant

Scale models of historic sailing ships are copied from detailed plans at La Marine

Dolly, and her husband, Douglas Bailey, who had arrived from the United Kingdom to work for Cable and Wireless, as a wedding gift. It was then that the verandahs on both sides of the house, as well as at the back, were added to the original construction. When Bailey died in 1972 during a visit to South Africa his wife decided to leave Seychelles, selling the estate, including the house and its furniture, to the Government.

Plans to build a craft village as a tourist, educational and cultural centre were conceived in 1977, but work on the old St Roch estate only started in 1985 after the United States agreed to finance the project. The Craft Village, now under the aegis of CODEVAR, took four years to complete. It consists of the totally refurbished plantation house, 12 exhibition spaces, and a restaurant designed to blend in with the architecture of the old house.

Some exhibition spaces act merely as shop windows for local craftspeople, while others serve as studio-cum-shops. The Craft Village houses Camille Poterie des Iles where a wide selection of pottery is produced and sold; Silver Tee's Design selling all sorts of T-shirts and clothes; a rattan blinds workshop; a small outlet selling La Marine products and a shop specialising in all things made from coconut including buttons, earrings and dolls.

British-born Elizabeth Rouillon, who uses her space as both a studio and shop arrived in Seychelles in 1983 and began operating out of the Craft Village in 1989. Trained in England in law, her botanical interests led her to become an artist once she had settled in Seychelles. She held her first solo exhibition in 1986. Naturally, Elizabeth's favourite subjects are local tropical plants, but she also paints tropical fish, landscapes and portraits. She works at home, but may also be found working directly from life in her studio at the Craft Village. She sells the majority of her original works — most, if not all, watercolours — from the studio, but her prints are also sold at a number of island outlets.

Soungoula ek Frere Torti, named after two characters from Seychellois folklore, is another of the craft shops. It is owned by John Etienne, a theatre director by profession who also works for the Ministry of Education and found time recently to publish his first book. Almost everything found in the shop is made from natural materials found in Seychelles. Traditional hats and bags woven from natural fibres are painted in bright colours, while small granite rocks, imaginatively covered in paint, make useful paperweights and are also attractive enough to stand as simple ornaments. The ubiquitous coconut is put to good use. There are 'dolls', made from the nut of a coconut; chunky bracelets made from the cut, hollowed shell of a coconut; and decorative candles made from wax-filled coconut shells. Watercolour paintings and models of traditional Seychellois houses are also on sale.

Carina is owned by a German woman, who produces hand-dyed shirts, sarongs, dresses and children's clothes in delicate shades of pink, orange, blue and green — perfect for hot, tropical days in the sun, as they are made from fine muslins and cool silks.

The Craft Village restaurant, Pomme Cannelle, housed in an open plan, traditionally styled house, serves Creole specialities including tuna steak, Millionaire's Salad, smoked fish salad, grilled lobster, crab in turmeric and coconut milk, fish curry and octopus salad. Evening meals are particularly enjoyable, the chandeliers shining overhead and the cool breeze running through the restaurant creating an elegant, yet informal setting. The restaurant caters for private functions, such as wedding receptions, business lunches and birthday celebrations.

To one side of the Craft Village driveway is a small thatched house known as the Coco House. Opened in 1992, the Coco House is a museum dedicated to the coconut palm and everything about it is made from that particular tree. On display are hats, traditional musical instruments, spoons, baskets, brooms, ropes and sculptures inside, as well as written details of the various uses for the coconut. Traditionally, young coconuts which fell from the palms, for example, were boiled in water and given to those suffering from diarrhoea; coconut roots were used to treat urinal disorders and dysentery; coconut oil was a treatment for constipation and is still used for cooking, and as a suntan oil.

Back on the South Coast Road, as you continue north with the sea on the right-hand side, the residential area of Turtle Bay is on the left. Beyond the turning to Montagnee Posee — one of the roads that leads back over the mountains to the west coast — and roughly one kilometre from the Craft Village at Val des Prés, in the district of Anse Aux Pins, is the national monument of the Lenstiti Kreol (Creole Institute). Built in the 19th century by a Mr France Jumeau on the occasion of his wedding, it is a large colonial house in a French architectural style which clearly reflects the opulence of the great property owners of that time. The spacious house and its solid walls were built using a vast amount of materials, most notably wood. A large verandah — the arched facade is edged with a decorative fascia border — runs around the entire ground floor and part of the first floor, which is now covered by a corrugated iron roof. Rattan blinds on the upper floor shield those inside against harsh weather conditions.

Since the time of France Jumeau the building has served many purposes. British Empire exiles once stayed in the property and in the 1960s it was a guesthouse under the name of Maison St Joseph. During the 1970s, the building started to fall into disrepair. It was not until 1989 that the building was renovated, with US Government funding. It took on its present role in October 1989. There are rumours that the building is haunted.

The main purpose of the Institute is to study the development of the Creole languages, in Seychelles and overseas, and to develop and coordinate the Seychellois dialect of the language. A recent addition to the Lenstiti Kreol is the construction of a traditional kitchen, built under the supervision of the National Archives in 1992 to mark the Kreol Festival in October of that year. It is on the existing foundations of the original kitchen.

Travelling further north, at the Casuarina Beach Hotel & Restaurant, which fronts the beach just to the south of Anse Aux Pins, the Creole restaurant specialises in seafood. The 12-room establishment offers snorkeling equipment, darts, a pool table and opportunities for fishing. Lalla Panzi, close to a souvenir shop, is a smaller guesthouse with only three rooms set in a

The nine-hole course at Reef Golf Club Hotel

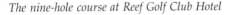

tropical garden close to the beach. Opposite, are the fairways of the only golf course in Seychelles. The nine-hole Reef Golf Club Hotel course was completed in 1971 and play began the following year. Initially, very much the domain of tourists and expatriates, now roughly one in five players is a Seychellois. Most golfers tend to play only nine holes for two reasons — because that is the length of the course and because of the heat, particularly in the middle of the day. Those intending to play are therefore recommended to start either in the early morning or in the late afternoon. Although not of international standard, the golf course will be appreciated by those who seek a little adventurous play and don't mind dodging the coconuts, which fall like ninepins from the plethora of palm trees that line the course.

The Reef Golf Club Hotel is located on the opposite side of the road from the course. One of the first modern hotels to open in Seychelles, it was inaugurated by the British Governor, Sir Bruce Greatbatch, in 1972. The hotel fronts the Anse Aux Pins Beach which is not good for swimming but provides excellent snorkeling. Other facilities offered at this 150-room property include two restaurants, two bars, a pizzeria, conference room, hairdressing salon and boutique. Sporting activities such as golf, tennis, badminton, jogging and a wide variety of watersports may all be arranged. Bicycles can be rented from the Reef Hotel, through Hercules Bicycle Hire, ring 373 039 for more details. Evening entertainment is provided by local bands, *sega* dancers and a disco.

Among the shops and offices of Anse Aux Pins is Victoria Car Hire, a small store that sells foodstuffs, the Blue Dolphin Club (a Democratic Party District Association Office) and a Stop'n'Shop general store, which also sells ice-cream. There is also a government health centre, a bus stop and police station, with two call boxes, one card-operated and one coin-operated outside. Behind the main bus stop is the village school, at the back of which, hidden at the end of a very rough dirt track in a verdant cul-de-sac several hundred metres from the main road, is the church of St Michael Archange. Not particularly impressive from the outside, the superb wooden ceiling inside — perhaps by accident, perhaps by design — seems like the inverted hull of some great fishing boat.

Opposite the playing fields of the school is a Relais des Iles known as La Retraite, which has just three rooms, all facing the sea. The guesthouse offers its residents Creole food and also sells crafts and souvenirs similar to those found at Soungoula ek Frer

Torti in the Craft Village. Anse Aux Pins also has a fish market, where fishermen bring their daily catch to be sold, but in reality it is little more than a landing station. In between La Retraite and the fish market, is the Voilier Art des Iles, a 'maquettes des bateaux' or model ship shop, where ships are on sale for up to SR35,000. The production methods vary from those at La Marine — just two people tend to work on one model, a man does the woodwork, while a woman fixes the sails and other attachments. On average, a pair of workers makes one model a week.

Opposite the fish market is the Savings Bank, next door to which is Anse Aux Pins District Council Office. There is also an SMB supermarket and a City Car Hire office, opposite Marvin's Video Shop and several general stores. A new housing development is on the edge of the village as you travel north. Right on the outskirts of the residential area is the Carefree Guesthouse and Restaurant. The closest accommodation to Seychelles International Airport, the Carefree has four rooms and a good restaurant which serves typical Creole food. Sitting in the restaurant it is possible to enjoy a nice sea breeze, but unfortunately the South Coast Road lies between the restaurant and the sea and there is a lot of traffic noise.

Around the corner, the deep bend of the road, Katiolo's restaurant specialises in seafood. It is better known, however, for its weekend disco, which is popular with the locals, particularly at the end of the month, around pay-day. Rounding the corner, the road rises and the far end of Seychelles International Airport's runway is visible. Returning to sea level, there is cultivated land to one side and the barracks of the Seychelles Coastguard on the other. Nearby is a general store and two call boxes, one card- and one coin-operated. There are several other general stores along this straight stretch of road. Between the road and the airport's runway is the Seychelles Bureau of Standards (SBS), next to which there is a rough track leading to the Helicopter Seychelles hangar. Those travelling on Helicopter Seychelles to outlying islands, however, must check in at the inter-island terminal at Seychelles International Airport.

Almost opposite is the Ministry of Planning and Development Home Ownership Scheme, Pointe Larue, where there are 100 self-help homes. There is also an ice-cream and candy store and the Pointe Larue District Council. Beryl's Ladies Fashionwear is close by. Beryl went to England to study fashion in London in 1979 and then gained invaluable overseas experience in fashion design, before her return home in 1991 to set up her own business. She now has two shops in town as well, where she sells her own creations and a few imported clothes. Although her main market is local, she does sell to tourists and will do 'one-offs' for special occasions such as spur-of-the-moment weddings. Opposite Beryl's store there is a mangrove swamp.

In the small industrial area to the left, the Amalgamated Tobacco Company (Seychelles) produce two brands of cigarette — Silhouette and Mahé Kings. Close by are an old yellowish-coloured plantation house and, opposite a petrol station, the entrance to Seychelles International Airport. When no international arrivals or departures are expected this small airport totally closes down. At other times the usual facilities, such as telephones, restaurant, car hire companies, banks and small shop are located within the airport complex. There is also a mini-market at the entrance to the airport where there is a coin-operated phone box.

Just north of the airport the village of Cascade is so named because of a stunning waterfall on Rivière Cascade high up the hillside. In *The Empire Review* of 1930 E Blackwood Wright reported that Cascade was one of the two places in Seychelles that a visitor must see. He wrote: 'The site of the cascade is most picturesque, situated about 800 feet up, between precipitous rocky walls forming an amphitheatre opening to the sea.' An old water wheel still exists, at the point where Rivière Cascade meets the original coastline and it does rotate after heavy rainfall. Just before the wheel, a steep side road leads to the church of Saint Andre, a tall, white building with lots of stained glass windows, a red roof and a distinctive pyramid-shaped steeple. The church towers over the village and looks out across the islands of the St Anne Marine National Park, while above it, granite mountain outcrops contrast with the rich green of the forest.

Next to the water wheel, back on the South Coast Road, is the Cascade Telephone Exchange. Adjoining this is the Centre Sosyal Cascade, the village social centre which has a basketball court, and opposite is the Cascade mini-market. There are several general stores between Cascade and Petit Paris, but the area is predominantly residential. A police housing estate on the right side of the road is easily recognisable because it is composed of yellow, three-storey buildings.

Opposite the Civil Construction Company, a sign marks the way to Tropicar, a car hire company. Take a right turn here to proceed along the new highway built out on the reclaimed land of the East Coast Project. By avoiding the congestion on the

Seychelles has one of the highest soft drink consumption levels in Africa

South Coast Road the road provides fast access to Victoria. It is a good route for bird-watching, as there is a bird sanctuary for migrant species near the Unity Stadium at Roche Caiman.

However, if you wish to see more of island life on the east coast of the island, stay on the old South Coast Road. There is another industrial zone along the road where there is a wide range of businesses. Sodepak produces soap, detergents and paper packaging products, as well as the coconut liqueur unique to the Seychelles, 'Coco d'Amour' which is attractively packaged in a *coco-de-mer* shaped bottle. Opposite Sodepak is the entrance to 'Souverains des Mers', another model ship factory. British Motors Seychelles, Penlac (a paint factory) and Seysteel are also found there and, along a short side road, a small craft workshop owned by Kreol d'Or produces 18-carat gold pieces for its shop in Camion Hall.

Next door to Kreol d'Or is Seychelles Creations, where thirty employees craft ceramics, shells and coconut shell into a wide range of goods including buttons, jewellery, belt-buckles and bags which they buy in and then decorate with shells. Prices vary between SR2 for a button and SR170 for a necklace. All the products are sold at the workshop and at a shop in Camion Hall,

Sundown over the Indian Ocean

while the buttons are exported to a number of countries, including Germany, France, Italy and Australia.

Almost next door is Seychelles Breweries, established in 1972 in partnership with a German brewery. This produces Guinness (under licence), Eku (under licence) and Seybrew, together with all the other bottled drinks, including Coca Cola, that are for sale on the islands.

The brewery has been a great success, which is not surprising when you see how much the Seychellois enjoy a bottle of beer and you learn that Seychelles has one of the highest soft drink consumption levels per capita in Africa. To protect the local environment, Seychelles Breweries operates a bottle deposit system in conjunction with its distributors and retailers.

Other businesses in the industrial zone include the Seychelles International Bank Agency; Universal Garage; Abhaye Valabjhi; Kobe Cars; Allied Builders and Aluminium Steel Works.

Not far beyond this industrial area, in the direction of Victoria, is one of the oldest, if not the very oldest surviving house in Seychelles, formerly known as Château de Mamelles. Built in 1804 for the corsair, Jean Francois Hodoul, it is now a private property and a national monument. Château de Mamelles was so named, because, in its original state, it resembled a small French château, but it has since been added to.

At one time it was believed that Hodoul built a tunnel which ran from the house, under the sea, to the island of St Anne which he used as a slave depot. This seems unlikely, as do the fantastic ghost stories told about the house.

The Michel Holiday Apartments share the same driveway as that of the former Château de Mamelles. These 16 self-catering apartments are well located as they are close to Victoria. Disadvantages include the noise which can be excessive as the apartments are close to the road and the lack of decent beaches anywhere nearby. Excursions and fishing trips can be arranged from the Apartments.

Just a little to the north, at the Bridge Shopping Centre, a small shop sells clothes and there is a well-stocked, modern, air-conditioned general store where phonecards may be bought. Next to the Centre, in the small car parking area, there are two call boxes — one card-operated, the other coin-operated — and a flight of stairs leads to the Les Mamelles Health Clinic.

Opposite the Bridge Shopping Centre is the office of Budget, a car rental company, and Galerie d'Art, the home, studio and gallery of local artist Gerard Devoud. A self-taught artist born in 1955 he wanted to paint from the time that he won a school art competition as a young boy. His first exhibition was held at the Pirate's Arms in 1974, at the tender age of 19 years. In 1977, his family moved to Europe, where he did receive some training, but, perhaps more importantly, came under the influence of artists such as Picasso, Van Gogh and Gauguin. Since the early 1980s, Gerard has been back in Seychelles, the one place in the world where he finds the inspiration for his brightly coloured paintings. Although his work has been compared with that of Michael Adams, Gerard's paintings are less detailed than those of his friend and sometime mentor, and more naive in nature. However, like Adams, he tends to reproduce the beauty of the Seychellois countryside with its lush vegetation, quaint traditional houses and magnificent seascapes. Gerard's favourite subject is the Vallée de Mai in Praslin. He has exhibited widely, both in Seychelles and in France, Switzerland, Italy, the United States and India. Gerard's largest exhibition was in Seychelles in 1988, when he exhibited a grand total of 72 paintings. He does sell his originals, but the silk-screen lithographs are much more affordable.

On the opposite side of the road, just past the Les Mamelles

Health Clinic, is Seypot, the Seychelles Potters' Cooperative. Established in 1981 by a group of graduates from the Seychelles Polytechnic, Seypot has been the breeding ground for the other potteries that have sprung up around the island. Seven potters work at Seypot, aged from 21 to 29 years. Some of them have trained at the Ceramic Centre in Mont Fleuri for three years, while others are under a Government scheme that sends young people into industries to train on the job. Initially, the pottery only produced simple items, such as vases and ashtrays, but now it has a whole range of items including wall plaques, plates, mugs and salt and pepper pots in the shape of tortoises. Several local hotels place large orders for bowls, plates, candleholders, ashtrays and vases. The clay used by Seypot comes from the clay unit at Val d'Endor. It is possible to watch the Seypot potters at work and then walk over to the small showroom where their products may be bought. Seypot products may also be purchased in hotel boutiques and various stores around town. Prices vary from SR13.25 for small vases rising to SR1,000 for a large ceramic tortoise.

Opposite Seypot, beyond a bus stop and basketball court, lies the *Isle of Farquhar*, a rusty old schooner which plied to and from the outer islands in better days, but now lies cut off from the sea by the land reclamation. On the left-hand side of the road are two Christian Fellowship meeting places and a general store. Then, after another general store housed in a modern, two storey building, a school and Plaisance District Council Office, you reach a roundabout. There, take a left-hand turn up La Misère Road if you wish to return to the west coast.

The road rises steeply at the beginning of La Misère Road past several general stores. The entrance to La Louise Lodge, a family-run guesthouse with just four rooms is on a sharp right-hand bend. Points in the lodge's favour include excellent views over the St Anne Marine National Park and a restaurant which serves both Creole and continental food.

A little further up the hill, on the same side of the road, is the Auberge Louis XVII, a fairly smart 10-room hotel set in tropical gardens which overlook the St Anne Marine National Park. Facilities include a swimming-pool and a restaurant serving continental and Creole cuisines.

Continue up the hill and stop at the viewing point to admire the panoramic view of the east coast of Mahé, from Victoria down almost as far as the Airport. From here, it is also easy to spot (with the aid of a ceramic map at the viewing point) many of the granite islands, particularly those in the St Anne Marine National Park. On Mahé itself, the glacis for which the granitic islands are famous, are close at hand.

The La Misère road continues to rise, passing a turning to the official residence of the French Ambassador. Along the same side road is Château Versailles, also known as Château Margot (the second of the two places that a visitor to Seychelles must see, according to E. Blackwood Wright in *The Empire Review* of 1930). A telephone exchange has now been built in front of Château Margot, which Wright described as 'a large villa on the summit of one of the mountains from which there is a marvellous view.

'It is built on the very ridge of the mountain. An hour's gallop on one of the island ponies lands you there. They are wonderful ponies who require neither spur nor whip to keep them going at break-neck speed up the hill path that leads through woods up to the pass near which Château Margot is built. Arrived at the top of the col, you see a wide open space some hundred yards long. At the end is the Château. A bath can be enjoyed in the big swimming-pool (the first in Seychelles) in the grounds before breakfast, and then you feast out of doors, with the wonderful blue all around you. Nearby is a steep cliff some thousand feet

Brighly coloured painting by local artist Gerard Devoud

sheer down from where the most wonderful sunsets are seen over the ocean.'

Further up La Misère, the road leads through a barrage of thick forest. Stop there for a quick roadside forage and marvel at the tree frogs and wild vanilla that climb along the mist-covered branches. Close to the crest of the hill, there is a well tarmacked road to the left which leads to the two 'golf balls' (as they are known locally, for that is what they resemble from afar) of the United States Satellite Tracking Station. Each 'golf ball' contains a satellite dish which is enclosed in a sphere to maintain the air-conditioning system necessary to keep the sophisticated equipment, which traces satellites and space shuttles, working properly. One dish collects the data and sends it across to the other, which relays the information into a geostationary satellite above the Atlantic Ocean. That satellite then beams the information to Washington, which re-transmits the information to a second geostationary satellite, and on to NASA headquarters at Cape Canaveral.

At the very crest of La Misère is a church. From there, the road starts to wend its way downhill to the west coast of the island. About a quarter of the way down the hill, on the right-hand side

The waterlily is a common coastal plant

of the road, is the entrance to the United States Tracking Station Base (their residential area). There are no more landmarks on this road, apart from the naturally stunning vistas of the west coast which take in Conception and Thérèse Islands from the road. The La Misère road finally reaches level ground at Grand Anse.

Back on the east coast, if, instead of taking the road to La Misère, you go straight across the roundabout and continue along the South Coast Road, there is a general store on the corner. The road then passes a playground, Adeline's Shop and Padayachy's Video store. Opposite the Mont Fleuri cemetery, there are two small general stores and a bedding shop.

Just past the cemetery is the Seychelles Police Traffic Section, opposite which is Photo Eden, a sister store to the shop of the same name in Victoria, which specialises in photographic equipment and has a one-hour film processing service. Next door to Photo Eden there is a bargain centre and two general stores, one of which sells phonecards which can be used at one of the two public call boxes opposite — the other is coin-operated. Mont Fleuri Police Station is also in the vicinity.

Cross over an outlet of the Rochon River (little more than a flue) and there is an upholstery shop and a general store on the left. Opposite is Jivan's Complex housing a video shop, general store and two clothing shops.

A little further along there is a turning to the International School of Seychelles. Opposite, is a general store run by Mrs M Chong Seng and just past that is La Moutia, a small, reasonably priced self-service cafe offering local curries, as well as Western fast foods like chicken and chips. The Beaufond Lane Guesthouse, with its convenient location within walking distance of Victoria, is on the same side of the road. The restaurant of this five-room Relais des Îles serves both continental and Creole cuisine.

On the left-hand side of the road, which is now known as Mont Fleuri Road, there is a general store and then the playing fields of the Seychelles Polytechnic. On the right, just past the building that used to accommodate the Regina Mundi Convent School for girls and which now houses government offices, there is Mont Fleuri District Council Office and Community Centre. The Convent, but not the school which no longer exists, has moved further along the road towards town.

There are many general stores along this section of the road and one which specialises in electrical and household goods. The 16-room, family-run Sunrise Guesthouse is also located in the vicinity. Although it has absolutely no view, the rooms are air-conditioned and it is conveniently located for town. On the left there is a turning to Hermitage where the Victoria Hospital is situated and then, continuing along the Mont Fleuri Road, past the Botanical Gardens, you find yourself back in town.

Additional Information

Lenstiti Kreol
Anse aux Pins
Mahé
Tel: 376 351
8am to 4pm Monday to Friday

La Marine
La Plaine St Andre
Mahé
Tel: 371 441
8am to 5pm Monday to Friday
8am to 3pm Saturday

Seypot
Les Mamelles
Mahé
Tel: 344 080
8am to 4pm Monday to Friday
8am to 12 noon Saturday

Galerie d'Art
Les Mamelles
Mahé
Tel: 344 280
8am to 8pm daily

Reef Golf Club
Anse Aux Pins
Mahé
Tel: 376 251
8am to 5pm daily

Craft Village
Anse Aux Pins
Mahé
Tel: 376 100
8am to 4pm Monday to Friday
8am to 5pm Saturday

Maison du Coco
Anse Aux Pins
Mahé
No telephone
9am to 5pm Monday to Friday
9am to 12 noon Saturday

5
OUTLYING ISLANDS

I sland hopping is an essential part of a visit to Seychelles if you really want to discover the full range of delights and attractions the 115 islands have to offer. Each one is as individual as the next in size, history, vegetation, wildlife and character. However, not all the islands are open to visitors, while some are little more than rocky outcrops in the sea. Many may only be reached by sea and are therefore restricted to yachts and ships. Others are closed for conservation reasons.

The most easily accessible islands are those close to Mahé which may easily be explored during a day, or even half a day, trip. Some islands, such as Thérèse, which lies off the west coast of Mahé, and Île Souris, close to Anse Royale, have already been covered in earlier chapters of this book. Another group, only mentioned in passing, is that within the St Anne Marine National Park, just off Victoria.

St Anne Marine National Park

The 15-square kilometre St Anne Marine National Park was established in March 1973. It is one of four marine national parks in the country administered by the Division of Environment, Conservation and National Parks Section of the Ministry of Environment, Economic Planning and External Relations.

The purpose of the park is to preserve the fragile marine ecosystem, on which hundreds of different species depend for survival. All the plants, corals, fish and other animals living in the sea, on the seabed and along the islands' shores up to 20 metres inland from the high water mark, are protected. The park's activities include the provision of breeding and nesting areas for endangered species such as turtles, research and monitoring of wildlife. At the same time, the park ensures the conservation of the beautiful coral reefs, sea plants, fish, birds and other wildlife in a natural state, so that they can be appreciated by both islanders and visitors.

The main coral is staghorn, recognisable by its trailing branches which resemble that of a tree. In water deep enough to sustain it, staghorn may grow as high as three metres. This particular coral provides a protective habitat for many of the 150-plus species of fish identified inside the park's boundaries, including butterfly fish, snappers and angel fish. Other corals to look for include the organ pipe, fire coral and a variety of soft corals.

An unusual feature of the park is the marine grass between the islands of Round and Cerf. Sandy patches provide a habitat for molluscs, starfish and small, burrowing shrimps. If you are lucky, you might also catch sight of green turtles and dolphins. At low tide, when the sand shallows are exposed, they become a resting and feeding place for sea and land birds such as green-backed herons, greenshanks, crab plovers, crested terns and noddies, which feast on crabs, worms and small fish.

Visitors may swim, snorkel, sail, laze on the beaches open to the public, ride in glass-bottom boats or semi-submersibles, dine in one of the Creole restaurants on Moyenne, Cerf or Round Islands or visit the park's Information Centre on Round Island. Naturally, fishing and the collection of shells and corals are forbidden. As they say, 'Take away nothing but photos and memories and leave only footprints.' Rangers patrol the park, assisting and informing visitors, while ensuring the protection of the marine life.

The park begins about three kilometres from Victoria Harbour and surrounds the six small islands of St Anne, Long, Moyenne, Cerf, Cachée and Round, plus their reefs. The park is accessible by boat — be it private, chartered or belonging to one of the local tour operators.

Charters may be organised through the Marine Charter Association in Victoria. The three main tour operators — Masons, National Travel Agency and Travel Services Seychelles — all organise day trips to the park which usually include a trip in a glass-bottom boat, a semi-submersible, an opportunity to snorkel and a Creole lunch on one of the islands.

St Anne

St Anne is the largest of the six islands within the boundaries of the park, occupying more than two square kilometres. It accommodates the Conservation and National Parks Section Headquarters and the Ranger Training Centre. As far as wildlife is concerned, St Anne is the most important nesting site within the granitic islands for hawksbill turtles, with a substantial number of females coming ashore at both Anse Cabot and Grande Anse in the north of the island.

Both St Anne and Long Island are owned by the government and neither is open to the public.

St Anne has an interesting history. In 1770, it was the site of the first permanent settlement in Seychelles, because Mahé was surrounded by impenetrable mangrove swamps at that time. In 1832, a whaling station was established on St Anne. The moorings for the slaughtered whales and a blubber boiler still exist at the southernmost tip of the island. During World War II, the British built a fuel storage facility on the west coast, still in use by the Seychelles Government, and used the island as a seaplane base. In addition, old gun emplacements still stand near the north-eastern shore. Between 1983 and 1991, a National Youth Service (NYS) camp occupied St Anne. Today, the light on the highest point (250 metres) acts as an important navigational aid to approaching aircraft.

Long Island

The other island closed to the public is Long Island. Covering an area of 21 hectares, the island houses a prison and quarantine station. In fact, Long Island has been a quarantine station for some time. The botanical artist, Marianne North, was forced to spend some time there in quarantine in 1883.

Cerf Island

Cerf is the second largest island in the St Anne Marine National Park, measuring almost two kilometres long and almost one kilometre wide. Its highest point rises to just 108 metres.

The island is named after the frigate, *Le Cerf*, which arrived in Victoria in 1756 with Captain Nicolas Corneille Morphey on board. It was he who claimed the islands for France by laying the Stone of Possession on Mahé.

The five-kilometre journey from Victoria direct to Cerf Island, which has a population of just 40, takes fifteen minutes by boat. Most visitors land on the north-east beach (the sea is calm all year round), disembark in shallow water and wade ashore. From the coast a trail leads across the island, through a forest inhabited by fruit bats, to the south-west coast. The trail branches to the north-west beach, where the offshore waters teem with marine life, and also continues around the southern headland back to the north-east coast. The island has two tiny disused chapels — one Anglican, the other Roman Catholic. Two restaurants on Cerf serve good Creole food — the Beach Shed Bar and Restaurant and the Kapok Tree.

Cachée (Île Cachée)

The island of Cachée lies off the south-east coast of Cerf. It is un-inhabited, but, as the name implies, many believe that treasure has been buried on the island.

Round Island

Just over five kilometres east of Victoria, Round Island is roughly a 15-minute boat ride from Victoria. As the island is less than 150 metres in diameter, the path which winds its way around the edge of Round Island may be walked in around 10 minutes.

The St Anne Marine National Park Information Centre, located on Round Island, provides interesting facts about the park's marine life and its protection, and is well worth a visit.

The only other objects of interest on the island are the rem-nants of a leper colony, which are located close to the pier. Prior to the 1930s, patients with mental problems were sent to Mauritius in return for Mauritian lepers. Originally, there was a house for the nursing staff, quarters for the lepers, a chapel and a small prison.

Today, the colony's chapel serves as the covered dining area of a restaurant, known as Chez Gaby, and the old prison cells house the restaurant's bar and kitchen. The restaurant, run by Mr and Mrs Calais who commute from their home on Cerf Island, is re-nowned for its excellent Creole food including specially marinated and barbecued tuna steaks, octopus and chicken cur-ries, salads, chutneys, followed by fresh fruit salad and caramelised coconut. Regular excursions to the island can be ar-ranged through Travel Services (Seychelles) Ltd on Mahé.

Moyenne

Just under half-a-kilometre long by quarter-of-a-kilometre wide, covering an area of nine hectares, Moyenne is probably the most beautiful of the islands in the St Anne Marine National Park.

The first visitors to the island are said to have been pirates, who reportedly left behind treasure worth around £30 million. The earliest traceable owner was Melidor Louange, who, in 1850, at the age of 17 married the 16-year-old Julie Chiffon. It is not known how they acquired Moyenne, particularly at so tender an age, but they were to live there until 1892, when they sold the island to Alfred d'Emmerez de Charmoy. He was said to be so wealthy that he lit his cigars with ten rupee notes — a handsome sum in those days. Seven years later, a woman from Berkshire, UK, by the name of Miss Emma Wardlow Best, moved in and stayed on the island until 1911.

Moyenne now belongs to retired newspaperman, Brendon Grimshaw, who is one of that lucky breed of people who find and buy their own deserted island. Yorkshire-born Brendon bought Moyenne several decades ago when he was working in East Africa. When he first moved to the island in the early 1970s, it had been deserted for about 60 years and was in a pathetic state of disrepair and decay.

Brendon's first job was to create a path around the island, which took him eight months. Since then, the island has been restored to its former glory and more by the introduction of some 7,000 endemic plants such as the *coco-de-mer*, Wright's gardenia and *bwa de fer*, all of which are labelled for the interest of visitors. In turn, the regeneration of the natural vegetation has led birds — roughly 1,000 of them — to return to the island. A number of giant tortoises also roam the island.

The first landmarks that visitors to Moyenne are likely to reach when they put ashore on the west coast of the island, however, are an old Creole villa where Brendon lives, the Jolly Roger Bar, an excellent place to sit and savour a cool drink, and Maison Moyenne, where excellent views of the park can be enjoyed while indulging in a sumptuous Creole meal.

From the landing point, it is possible to follow the trail created by Brendon, which takes between 40 minutes to an hour to complete. The path leads through the forested interior, past two ruined houses — one previously occupied by the Louange family and the other, known as the House of Dogs, by Miss Best. The

The first visitors to Moyenne Island are thought to have been pirates

second house was given its name because Miss Best used to bring stray dogs from Mahé to be looked after on Moyenne. So attached was she to animals, that when she died, she left the island to two friends on the condition that nothing 'not even a rat' was to be killed.

The small cemetery on the island, mentioned in documents dating from 1892, has just three graves. Two are thought to be 18th-century pirate graves, while the third is that of Raymond Grimshaw, Brendon's father, who died on 31 January 1986 and whose epigraph remembers him as 'father and friend'. There are also said to be ghosts on the island: Brendon tells of windows and doors banging without cause, beds being shaken and the sound of people marching at midnight from the cemetery to the Creole villa and back again. Brendon also relates the tale of when he heard a voice urge him to go to Coral Cove (on the island) at four o'clock in the afternoon of the following day to see a turtle come out of the sea and lay her eggs. Sure enough, the next day he went to the cove and the turtle appeared to lay her eggs at exactly the time predicted.

Moyenne's northern coast is the best place from which to explore the underwater world, for the waters between St Anne and Moyenne are recognised as the best snorkeling grounds in the park. The fish most commonly seen in this area are butterfly fish and red soldier fish, but the nearby reef is home to more than 150 different species, so be prepared to see a lot more.

Silhouette

Silhouette, the third largest island in Seychelles, lies 19 kilometres off the north-west coast of Mahé. Roughly round in shape, it extends five kilometres in length and five kilometres across to encompass 20 square kilometres of syenite. This differs substantially from that of the other pre-Cambrian granitic islands, as it was formed more recently, in the Tertiary period.

Standing on Mahé's Beau Vallon Bay, it is easy to imagine how the island may have got its name. The silhouette of the island etched against the evening sky is a prominent part of Seychelles' scenery. However, the island was named after an 18th-century French minister.

It is not known who were the first people to land on Silhouette, which is difficult to reach by sea because it is encircled by an almost continuous reef that serves as a deterrent to all but the most daring of sailors. Finds of pottery on Silhouette's mountainside have led to claims that Indonesian migrants on their way to Madagascar in the 12th century may have stopped off on the island for a season in order to grow crops, replenish their supplies and repair their boats. These claims, however, remain unsubstantiated. As does the story of the Indian sailors (or were they Arabs?) who are said to have been shipwrecked at Anse Lascar and who stayed there for a few years, leaving their graves as evidence. Given that a Lascar is a sailor from East India, it is more likely that they were from the sub-continent. According to local legend, the well-known French pirate Jean Francois Hodoul, also lived on Silhouette, burying much of the treasure that he captured somewhere on the island.

The first sure settlement on the island took place towards the end of the 18th century when a family by the name of d'Auban (later spelt Dauban) emigrated from Mauritius to the island. Slowly, the Dauban family bought up different parts of Silhouette, until eventually they owned it all. Under their ownership, agriculture became the mainstay of the economy, with copra, cinnamon, patchouli and fruit, the main crops grown. With all this agriculture, the population peaked at 1,000 in the 1950s.

As agriculture was the only form of commercial activity on the island until 1987, development has been slow and leisurely and the island has not changed much. Consequently, many consider Silhouette to be one of the most physically beautiful and least spoilt islands in the entire granite group.

The only other commercial development on the island since its opening in 1987, is Silhouette Island Lodge, a 12-bungalow hotel, where the facilities include a restaurant serving good Creole and Italian food and a watersports centre. Both SCUBA diving and snorkeling are popular just off Silhouette as the numerous reefs contain a multitude of fish and shells which have remained largely untouched by marine pollution or human depredation. Deep-sea fishing from the island is also recommended as the fishing grounds just off Silhouette are excellent for catches of sailfish, tuna, bonito, barracuda and mackerel. The bungalows, each with its own private bathroom, hot and cold running water and electricity, stretch along the beach. The diversification of the island's interests came about through the failure of agriculture and the depopulation of the island as inhabitants left for Mahé in search of better paid jobs, reducing the population to its present 200. Most have spent their life on the island.

The lodge is located on the east coast of Silhouette, at Anse La Passe, the largest settlement. Anse La Passe includes La Grande

Case, an old, beautifully preserved colonial-style planter's house, built from takamaka wood in the 1860s by August Dauban. According to folklore, he bought the land on which it stands for a Stradivarius violin. It is true that August was a French infantry captain who fought for Napoleon at the Battle of Waterloo, but the Stradivarius story is an embellishment — he actually paid 4,000 silver coins and a Malagasy fiddle to the previous owner who, it is said, could make the fiddle sound like a Stradivarius.

Silhouette is a walker's paradise. There are no vehicles. Paths cross the island through dense forest which, even today, still reveals rare or unique plant and animal species. Due to the lack of development, Silhouette has also retained much more of its original vegetation, particularly at 400 metres and above sea level, than other islands. In fact, it is one of the thickest virgin forests in the Indian Ocean.

 A walk from La Passe over the mountain to the west coast leads through sylvan reserves of sandalwood, giant albizzia and cinnamon trees. A species of pitcher plant, found only in Seychelles, grows here and there are also many endemic species of orchids. The trail over the hill splits high above La Passe, but both trails lead down into the west coast settlement of Grande Barbe. The walk is no mere stroll in the park. Silhouette rises from the submerged plateau of the Seychelles Bank, to a height of 740 metres above sea level. In fact, so steeply does it rise that during the rainy north-west monsoon, spontaneous waterfalls appear on its slopes.

A full day should be set aside to really savour the beauty of this walk across the island. The path is steep in places, but it is easily followed as the islanders commute regularly between Grande Barbe and La Passe and have left a well-trodden trail. One of the island's few churches is situated in Grande Barbe, overlooking a magnificent beach. Silhouette's largest river, the Seme, also feeds into the sea at Grande Barbe.

From Grande Barbe it is possible to follow another trail along the west coast to Anse Mondon in the north, where there is another trail which returns, via the east coast, to La Passe. The scenery en route is totally wild. Rugged cliffs give way to remote, long, sandy beaches. There has been no sporadic building outside the settlements, so you really feel as if you are on a deserted island.

One more trail leads south from La Passe to Anse Lascar and beyond. At Pointe Ramasse Tout, which is just south of La Passe, it passes close to the impressive but neglected mausoleum of the

Dauban family. The remains of August, his wife — an intelligent, combative woman descended from the same family in Ireland that produced J F Kennedy's forebears — and two daughters are interred in this miniature copy of Paris's Eglise de la Madeleine. All are commemorated by worn marble tablets, inscribed with meditations upon the death of Socrates. Shrouded in lush tropical vegetation, the grandeur of this monument speaks volumes for the wealth of the plantation aristocracy.

Not only wealth, but also character. August's grandson, Henri, was born on Silhouette and grew up there as a young boy. One of his favourite pastimes was harpooning fish. Sent to boarding school in England, he later graduated from the London School of Economics where, in 1924, he watched a group of men throwing javelins. To Henri, the javelins were the same as harpoons which he knew he could throw better and he asked if he might try. Without a run, he hurled the javelin twice the distance of any others and within weeks was in Paris, competing in the 1924 Olympics.

The quickest and most convenient way to reach Silhouette today is by Helicopter Seychelles, which operates a shuttle service between the island and Seychelles International Airport on

Silhouette Island rises to a height of 740 metres above sea level

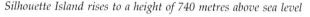

Mahé. The Boat House at Beau Vallon on Mahé, however, also operates sea trips to Silhouette.

Frégate

Just 20 residents occupy the two square kilometres of Frégate, the most isolated of Seychelles' granitic islands. Just under two kilometres long and a little more than a kilometre wide, Frégate lies 55 kilometres east of Mahé and is a 15-minute flight from the main island.

Frégate's relative isolation has given rise to countless tales of buried treasure: 18th-century pirates are said to have based themselves there, but no one can be sure. Stories of treasure include a large chest containing Spanish coins, axes, swords, knives, Dutch pikes and crockery. In 1812, a cross belt and shoulder strap of gold are said to have been discovered. At Grand Anse are the remains of buildings, cannonballs and a well lined with lead, which may have some association with pirates, if not early Arab sailors.

Aside from pirates, the first known record of Frégate comes from the journal of Lazare Picault, penned during his second voyage of exploration from Mauritius in 1744. Picault's vessel reached Seychelles via the Chagos Archipelago and anchored off Frégate, as it was the first landfall. It was probably Picault who named the island Île aux Frégates, because of a significant presence of frigatebirds. The next documented visit to Frégate was made by Jean Baptiste de Malavois in 1786. He reported that, unlike the other granite islands, there were no crocodiles on Frégate, but there were giant tortoises, turtles and dugongs (sea cows). In 1802, Louis Francois Sepholet and three slaves were exiled to Frégate. The former was involved in an attempt on the life of Napoleon and the slaves were said to have been planning an uprising. However, they were removed by the Mauritian authorities before the end of the year and taken to the Comores.

Nowadays, visitors to Frégate stay in the comfortable surroundings of The Plantation House, the only hotel on the island, which has just ten rooms and is thus able to provide a very personalised service. The hotel, as romantic as the legendary stories surrounding the island, is reached through an archway formed by the aerial roots of a giant banyan tree. Under its leafy shade a bird-table attracts dozens of birds in search of titbits left by guests. The Creole cuisine served in the hotel's restaurant is prepared from food grown on the island. Bananas, papaya, chillis, sweet potatoes and many other vegetables are all cultivated close to the guesthouse. The Plantation House has no watersports centre as such, but, depending on weather conditions, big-game fishing can be arranged.

There are no vehicles, so the island must be explored on foot. The only beach on the south side of the island, Anse Parc, is just a short and pleasant stroll from The Plantation House, through woodlands and diminishing plantations. The sandragon tree is the most dominant woodland tree on the island, but breadfruit, banyan and wild cashew trees have replaced much of the indigenous vegetation, although a number of takamaka trees remain.

Rather than walking straight on to Anse Parc, take the path to the right, which leads around the island to the west coast and the sparkling beaches of Petite Grande Anse and Grand Anse. Continuing north along the trail, the path keeps close to the coast and eventually leads to Anse Victorin — one of the three northern beaches. The others are Anse Maquereau and Anse Bambous. From Anse Victorin, the path takes an inland route back to The Plantation House.

Another cross-country footpath from the hotel leads west up the slopes of 125-metre-high Mount Signal, which dominates the island, to a point just four metres below the summit and from there it is possible to look westwards across the ocean to Mahé.

On your walks around the island, look out for various indigenous fauna. The extremely rare Seychelles magpie robin is unique to Frégate and, although once common throughout the granite islands, is now close to extinction with only about 45 birds remaining. However, by improving the habitat on Frégate and transferring birds to other islands such as Aride, Bird Life International plans to save the magpie robin. The handsome black and white bird is a member of the thrush family. Its song is melodious, often delivered from prominent positions, such as the top of a palm tree. It is this characteristic that gives the bird its Creole name 'ti santez' or 'little singer'.

Other birds to look out for include the Seychelles fody, which is only found there and on two other islands, Cousin and Cousine. The male fody has a yellow head when in breeding plumage, while the female and non-breeding males are dark brown. Frégate also boasts one of the densest populations of the Seychelles blue pigeon. The beautiful fairy tern, the most common breeding seabird, is always to be seen on Frégate.

Another inhabitant unique to Frégate is the giant tenebrionid beetle which, despite its knobbly wing-cases cannot fly and is

Sunworshippers enjoy fabulous Anse Victorin on Frégate
Opposite: Anse Victorin beach, Frégate

usually seen clinging to the flanks of the sandragon trees. Its long legs are its other most distinctive feature. Interestingly, it is alleged that when this insect was first described in scientific terms, the writer was accused of fraud, for combining the descriptions of several different insects. Nocturnal scorpions, caecilians (blind, legless amphibians), giant land tortoises, green geckos and lizards also live on Frégate.

The easiest way to reach Frégate is by one of the daily Air Seychelles flights from Mahé to the landing strip on the north-eastern coast of the island. At certain times of the year, however, it is also possible to reach Frégate by boat, particularly from Praslin.

Additional Information

St Anne Marine National Park Information Centre, Round Island
Tel: 224 644 (Ministry of Environment, Economic Planning and External Relations, Division of Environment, Conservation and National Parks Section), 8am to 4pm Mondays, Wednesdays, Thursdays, Saturdays and Sundays.

6
PRASLIN

Praslin is the most popular destination away from Mahé, for one simple reason. The island's Vallée de Mai is one of the country's two World Heritage Sites and one of only two places — the other is the nearby island of Curieuse — in the world where the *coco-de-mer* is found growing naturally. In addition, as the second largest island in the archipelago, it has a regular air and sea service and a good number of hotels, to cope with large numbers of tourists.

Twelve kilometres long by five kilometres wide, Praslin lies 45 kilometres north-east of Mahé and covers 37 square kilometres. The highest point on the island is Fond Azore in the south-west.

Lazare Picault made the first known landing on Praslin in 1744 when he named it 'Île de Palme' (Palm Island), in recognition of the *coco-de-mer* and five other rare, endemic palms which grow on the island. In 1768, just before the first settlement in Seychelles was established on St Anne, Marion Dufresne visited the island, placed a deed of possession in a bottle and buried it at Anse Possession on the northern coast directly opposite Curieuse. At that time Île de Palme was renamed Praslin, in honour of the celebrated Duc de Praslin, a French minister of state who was later guillotined.

From 1810, when only ten families lived on Praslin, the island slumbered dreamily through most of the century. In 1846, Charles Pridham wrote: 'The anchorage is good and safe towards the north between it and Île Curieuse, and the tide rises six or seven feet. The population amounted to 408 in 1825, of whom 30 families were French. The soil is excellent in the valleys, and even in elevated places, and well adapted for the growth of cotton. The hard wood, with which the hills are clothed, proves excellent timber. Cocoa trees are plentiful in the valleys.' The most note-worthy event in the 19th century was the visit of General Charles Gordon in 1881. The hero of Khartoum was sure that he had found the Garden of Eden and declared the *coco-de-mer* to be the biblical tree of knowledge.

In the 20th century, however, Praslin has taken great strides forward, particularly since the development of tourism, but it still retains a friendlier atmosphere and slower pace of life than Mahé. The opening of the airport in Amitié in 1975 brought the island into the air age and has really helped to open the island up to tourism which is now the cornerstone of Praslin's economy. However, attempts are being made to diversify and a boatyard has been opened at Baie St Anne, the largest settlement on Praslin and the point from where most schooners ply between Mahé and the neighbouring island of La Digue. From very early in the morning, the port of Baie St Anne bustles with activity as the schooners leave for Mahé at dawn, or earlier. For the rest of the day, this natural port on the east of the island is busy with schooners which constantly ferry tourists and workers to and from La Digue.

The schooners arrive back at Baie St Anne from Mahé early in the afternoon. Whether travelling to Praslin by boat or air, visitors are likely to end up at Baie St Anne for it is the island 'capital' with banks, shops, hospital, church and a monument to the *coco-de-mer*. Travelling south from Baie St Anne, along the coast where there are many small jetties and moorings, take the first road to the right (straight on will bring you to the schooner pier) and up a very steep hill with a triple hairpin bend.

At the top of the climb, there is an excellent view of Baie St Anne, one of the most scenic natural harbours in Seychelles, and indeed, the world. Continue along the road which dips and rises with alarming frequency, particularly if travelling by bicycle. Château des Feuilles, one of the most exclusive hotels in Seychelles, is on the left-hand side, at Pointe Cabris. This 12-room establishment is located on a hilltop amidst extensive gardens. Facilities include a swimming-pool, a restaurant specialising in seafood and excursions to neighbouring islands.

There is a small settlement at Anse Consolation and another steep hill as the road continues on towards the west coast of Praslin. After this, the road is much more level although, in parts, unsurfaced as it passes many secluded beaches such as Anse Bois de Rouge, Anse Takamaka, Anse Bateau and Anse Citron. On the beach front at Anse St Sauveur there is an art

Schooners moored at the tiny harbour on Praslin

school, Cresswell Art Holidays, where visitors can stay and study art, if they wish. Artists and would-be artists must, however, bring all their own materials with them on holiday as they are not available in Seychelles. In general, the west side of the island is wilder than the east side; the beaches are small and the reef is closer to the shore, making swimming difficult.

When the road finally reaches a junction, take the road to the left, along the coast to Grande Anse, another large settlement, little more than a kilometre along the road. On the north-west coast, the three-and-a-half kilometres of gleaming sand that is Grande Anse looks out over Cousin, one of Praslin's satellite isles. Although there is a beautiful beach, the tides bring in vast quantities of seaweed and the shallow water over the coral makes swimming difficult at low tide.

Nevertheless, Grand Anse is the island's most developed resort with a church, school, police station, shops and restaurants. Entering the village, the church is on the right-hand side. Turning a sharp corner, there is a 'take-away', highly recommended both for its excellent food and value for money, opposite the settlement's small market. Carry on through the village and the first hotel you reach, on the left-hand side, is

Grande Anse Beach Villas. This is a small, friendly hotel with eight palm-thatched chalets just metres from the beach. This family-run hotel normally provides bed and breakfast only, but other meals will be prepared on request. Just a little further along the coast is the Indian Ocean Fishing Club. The facilities at this 16-room hotel include a restaurant serving both international and Creole cuisines, evening entertainment such as local bands and dance troupes, big-game fishing and a swimming-pool. Continue along the road and the property of the Flying Dutchman, one of the oldest hotels on Praslin, straddles the road. Guests, housed in 13 thatched bungalows, can enjoy a beach-front restaurant serving international and Creole cuisines, evening shows, big-game fishing and excursions to a number of Praslin's satellite islands.

The road then passes through the village of Amitié, where there is a school and church. Maison des Palmes, a 16-room ho- tel, is located on the beach front, just past the village. It offers visitors a Creole restaurant, swimming-pool, facilities for sailing, windsurfing and big-game fishing, as well as yacht charters to neighbouring islands. Carry on along the road and you will pass the end of the runway. Take the first right to reach the airport terminal, which offers a lounge with a shop for departing pas- sengers, as well as housing Praslin's Tourist Information office. The airport is built on the Amitié Estate, the rest of which is agricultural land.

Back on the main road, the route leads to the picturesque sandy beach of Anse Kerlan, lined by casuarina trees. Do not be tempted by its beauty during the north-west monsoon, however, when strong winds and powerful currents make it dangerous for swimmers.

At Anse Kerlan the road continues straight on to the beach with a right turn towards the hillside. Take the right turn, and start a long, rough ride to Anse Lazio, the most beautiful beach on the island. Two hundred metres along this road, a turn left leads to the Islander Guesthouse, a small self-catering establishment consisting of two chalets, each with two apartments. The north end of beautiful Anse Kerlan is no more than 10 metres from the chalets. As you carry on along the unpaved path to Anse Lazio, a steep paved path rises at the right-hand side with bushes of red Barbadian cherries on either side. Take this path and where the road levels out, there is a typical Seychellois house on the left. The road then carries on, passing woodland where vanilla plants cling to trees, up to the crest of the hill. From now on, it's all downhill with stunning views across open waters to the island of Aride before Anse Lazio appears to the right, on the fringe of protective Chevalier Bay. The red earth road that has been followed ends abruptly at a house painted turquoise blue. From there, take a steep path down to the beach — you will have to carry your bicycle at this stage. Anse Lazio, on the north-west tip of the island, is famous for its excellent swimming and snorkeling. There is a restaurant close to the beach, for those in need of a thirst-quenching drink.

From Anse Lazio, the road rises steeply to the crest of a hill and then gently descends to Anse Boudin, where scenes of typical village life may be observed. Curieuse lies just offshore. The sea between Praslin and Curieuse and Curieuse itself are all part of the Curieuse Marine National Park.

From Anse Boudin, along the northern coast, the road rolls past Anse Takamaka and Anse Possession. On the left-hand side, at Anse Petite Cour, there is a turning to La Reserve, which was once little more than a guesthouse, but has now expanded and earned a reputation for itself as a top-class hotel. The suites in this 16-room hotel are said to be the most luxurious on the island and are furnished with antiques as well as modern amenities such as telefax machines. The restaurant, serving international, Chinese and Creole cuisines, is rightly famous for its excellent food. There are also facilities for tennis, snorkeling, big-game fishing, SCUBA diving and there is a watersports centre just three minutes away by car.

Continue along the main road and Anse Volbert, where there is another magnificent beach, is not far. Four kilometres in length, Anse Volbert is a beautiful, if relatively crowded beach, popularly known as the Cote D'Or. Several hotels line the beach. The 80-room Paradise Sun, which has recently been renovated, is set in a lush tropical garden. The large rooms all have a private bathroom, en suite dressing room and verandah. Facilities include a main dining-room, Le Beach Restaurant (situated right on the beach which only serves meals during the day) and two bars. There is a daily programme of events including boat excursions, hiking trips, snorkeling, volleyball, petanque, table tennis, billiards and a variety of indoor games. Evening entertainment is based on various themes and a number of local bands play there.

The nearby Praslin Beach Hotel has 76 rooms set in a tropical garden. The hotel has a well-equipped watersports centre, with Hobie Cats, windsurfers, canoes, pedaloes, snorkeling equipment and opportunities to learn to SCUBA dive.

Also on the beach at Anse Volbert is Café des Arts, an art gal-

lery-cum-restaurant established by well-known local painter,
Christine Harter who studied in Britain in the late 1970s and returned home to capture typical scenes of Seychelles life in pastel
shades of watercolours. Aside from her own work, many other
local artists are featured in the gallery.

At the southernmost end of Anse Volbert, a small secluded
cove called Anse Gouvernement boasts the hotel L'Archipel. Sixteen luxuriously appointed rooms all have sea views, television,
private verandah and private bathroom. The watersports include
canoeing, snorkeling, windsurfing, SCUBA diving, deep-sea fishing and bottom fishing. Lunch is served at the Beach Bar, dinner
in the main restaurant and, once a week, there is live music. Children under the age of three are not allowed to stay at the hotel.

From Anse Volbert, the road leads in a southerly direction to a
T-junction at Anse Madge. Take a left turn to visit the smaller of
the two Grand Anses on Praslin or a right turn to return to Baie
St Anne. In the midst of the island capital, take a right turn towards the larger Grand Anse. The road rises to cross the hill and,
higher up, on the right hand side, is the entrance to the Vallée de
Mai.

When General Gordon visited Praslin in 1881 and wandered
through the Vallée de Mai he thought he had discovered the
original Garden of Eden. He devised the Seychelles coat of arms
with its *coco-de-mer* palm standing on a giant tortoise. A snake
entwined around the palm signifies Eden. The coat of arms has
been retained by the republic, but not the snake.

The *coco-de-mer*, Gordon believed, was the tree of knowledge
used to test Adam and Eve. Its fruit, he wrote, 'externally represents the heart, while the interior represents the thighs and belly,
which I consider as the true seat of carnal desires. . .'

When the nuts were washed ashore on other islands and continents, they were thought to have come from large submarine
trees, hence the name *coco-de-mer* (sea coconut). They inspired
many legends. The Indonesians thought the tree might be the
home of the mythical garuda bird and the Indians attributed special healing powers to the nuts. Several of the nuts were made
into drinking vessels, decorated in gold and silver, by European
rulers and can now be found in various museums, including the
British Museum.

Because of the nuts' voluptuous feminine shape, some people
believed they had aphrodisiac qualities. The elders of Praslin still
hold that they do, if you soak the kernel of the nut overnight and
boil it for drinking. To add to the sexy nature of the tree,

propogation is said to only take place when the female tree, which bears the nuts, is close to the male tree, which has a phallus-shaped long, brown dangling catkin. Local folklore is full of stories about people cursed for looking at or hearing the trees mate. Insects or the wind are probably responsible for pollination; geckos may also transport pollen.

The *coco-de-mer* palm grows naturally only on Praslin and Curieuse. The palm starts to bear fruit after 25 years and it takes seven years for a nut to mature. The trees can then live up to 200 years. Some of the ones in the Vallée de Mai are 45 metres high. In the park there are many hollow 'bowls' in the ground — the sites of dead palms which may last many decades after the tree has fallen.

There are approximately 4,000 palms in the Vallée de Mai. The female palm produces about 20 nuts. They each weigh up to 20 kilograms, making them the heaviest seed in the world. The younger, green nuts can be eaten when they are a year old. The mature ones may be bought either whole, cut in half sideways to make fruit bowls, or cut into four to make good serving bowls.

Also look out for the rare black parrot, which is found only on Praslin and Curieuse. Fewer than 100 of the dark brown birds live on Praslin.

Praslin may be reached either by air or by sea. The 'Praslin taxi' — an Air Seychelles Twin Otter which flies between Mahé and the airstrip at Amitié in Praslin roughly nine times a day (depending on demand) — is certainly the quickest route, taking only 15 minutes. Otherwise, local schooners leave the ferry pier in Victoria around noon to arrive in Baie St Anne, the main settlement on Praslin, three hours later. The schooner is an interesting way to travel during the north-westerly monsoon, but the voyage is often rough during the south-easterlies. Day trips are organised by most tour operators.

Additional Information

Vallée de Mai Praslin, 8am to 5pm daily

The Vallée de Mai was reputed to be the original Garden of Eden

7
PRASLIN'S SATELLITE ISLANDS

Praslin has four satellite islands of importance — Cousine, Cousin, Curieuse and Aride. Privately owned Cousine is not open to the public; the other three do not have tourist accommodation and are open only to day-trippers.

Cousin and Aride, both under the auspices of the Royal Society for Nature Conservation, are an ornithologist's delight and rank among the most important bird sanctuaries in the world. Curieuse, as the terrestrial element of the Curieuse Marine National Park, plays an important role in the country's conservation programme.

Curieuse

Curieuse, which covers a total of three square kilometres, lies one kilometre from the northernmost point of Praslin and about 52 kilometres from Mahé. The island is about three-and-a-half kilometres long by two-and-a-half kilometres (at its widest point). The highest point, Mount Curieuse, rises 172 metres.

Originally called 'Île Rouge' (Red Island) because of the exposed red earth, which is still a feature of the island, it was renamed Curieuse in 1768 when Marion Dufresne paid a visit aboard the schooner *La Curieuse*. The sailor Dufresne was impressed by the lush vegetation — including *coco-de-mer* trees — that he saw. Since fire ravaged its forests and laid bare the hillsides, Curieuse is starting to bloom again thanks to a recent reafforestation programme. Large takamaka and casuarina trees shade some beaches, while mango, banana, orange, mandarin and jackfruit trees grow inland. Giant tortoises have been introduced from Aldabra in an attempt to establish a colony. Bird species found there include the Seychelles sunbird, the Seychelles bulbul and the fairy tern.

Curieuse, along with the entire channel between the island and Praslin, and a large section of Praslin's northern shoreline, is part of the Curieuse Marine National Park. The park accounts for 14 square kilometres of marine and terrestrial environment.

Visitors to Curieuse land close to the Turtle Pond, a small lagoon created by a man-made, stone causeway across the mouth of Laraie Bay. The lagoon was stocked with turtles, which were caught and kept there prior to export. From the landing stage, a trail cuts across to Anse St Jose on the south coast, the best beach on the island, which is protected by a coral reef. The pathway leads past the ruins of an old leper colony established on the island in 1833. A large house nearby was reserved for the doctor when he came from Praslin. Further along the coast is a small cemetery.

The other trail from the landing stage runs along the edge of the Turtle Pond, through a mango plantation to cut across the interior of the island, under Mount Curieuse, to Anse Badamier on the north coast.

Since there is no accommodation, Curieuse opens on Tuesdays, Thursdays and Fridays from 0900 to 1600 and on Sundays from 0900 to 1200, all year round. Hotels and tour operators in Praslin arrange boats.

Cousin

Cousin Island, one of the smaller granitic islands, measures under a kilometre long by about half-a-kilometre wide. It covers just 28 hectares. Its highest point above sea level is 58 metres. It lies roughly 44 kilometres from Mahé and under three kilometres from Praslin's west coast.

Cousin is a great conservation success. In 1959, the Seychelles warbler was on the brink of extinction — only 26 were left in the world. Through the early 1960s, the destruction of the original forest cover for the commercial planting of coconuts and cotton contributed to the bird's decline. Other birds, such as the wedge-tailed shearwater, were also caught for food while hawksbill turtles were killed for their shells and green turtles for their meat. On the reefs, shells disappeared steadily. In other words, Cousin was plundered.

In 1968 the Royal Society for Nature Conservation (RSNC), with help from the World Wildlife Fund (WWF) and Christopher Cadbury bought the island. Since then, it has become a sanctuary for endangered species, managed by Bird Life International. In 1975, the Government lent its support to the project, declaring the island a Special Reserve.

Under the protection of the RSNC and Bird Life, native woodland, including indigenous coastal trees such as *Morinda* and *Pisonia*, has been encouraged to regenerate. As a result, the Seychelles warbler population has grown substantially — to more than 400 in 1990. It now has been taken off the Red Data list of threatened species.

The only path on the island leads from the western beach of Anse Vacoa, along the northern coast of the island, to a much larger, unnamed beach on the north-eastern shore. The path then heads inland.

The Seychelles warbler is not the only bird to flourish under the watchful eye of Bird Life. Other birds include the Seychelles

fody or 'tok tok' which has disappeared from all but three islands, the Seychelles sunbird, the Seychelles blue pigeon, the wedge-tailed shearwater (which breeds on Cousin between October and March), the Audubon's shearwater, the fairy tern, the white-tailed tropicbird, the lesser noddy, the brown noddy and the bridled tern. In all, Cousin supports more than a quarter-of-a-million breeding seabirds.

Other wildlife has benefited from the creation of this Special Reserve. If you are lucky, and visit Cousin between the months of August and April, you may also catch sight of a hawksbill turtle. The islands' beaches remain an important breeding ground in the western Indian Ocean for this endangered species, due to a lack of predators and vigilant protection.

Interesting flora to keep an eye out for include the tortoise tree (*Morinda*), the fruit bat tree and the endemic Balfour's pandanus.

As a special nature reserve, Cousin is only open on Tuesdays, Thursdays and Fridays, with guided tours. These may be booked through most hotels and travel agents on Praslin. The best months for visiting the island are between April and September. Please note that certain rules and regulations must be observed on Cousin. Swimming, shell collecting, smoking and picnics are all forbidden.

Aride

The most northerly granite island in Seychelles is Aride, 50 kilometres north-east of Mahé and 16 kilometres from Praslin. One-and-a-half kilometres long by a little more than half-a-kilometre wide, the island covers 68 hectares and rises to 'Gros La Tete', 135 metres above sea level.

First discovered in 1756, Aride was so named because of its lack of fresh water. It enjoyed a relatively quiet life — pirates are thought to have used the island as a refuge in the 17th and 18th centuries. After a century of ownership by the Chenard family, who had declared the island a private nature reserve, it was bought, in 1973, by Christopher Cadbury on behalf of the Royal Society for Nature Conservation (RSNC). In June 1975, Aride was made a Special Reserve under Seychelles law.

Today, Aride is considered of global importance as home to the world's largest colony of the lesser noddy and possibly the white-tailed tropicbird. Figures for the lesser noddy colony speak for themselves. In 1955, there were an estimated 20,000 pairs on the island; by 1988, that figure had grown to 170,000 and, eventually, experts believe that figure could reach 250,000. Nowhere else on earth is it possible to find a rocky hillside covered with nesting sooty terns. It is the only breeding site in the granite islands for roseate terns and red tailed tropicbirds, while the beautiful, fragrant Wright's gardenia (Aride is the only home of this flowering shrub) grows nearby.

Aride has more species of breeding seabirds than any other island in Seychelles except Aldabra. Apart from the massive numbers of lesser noddies and white-tailed tropicbirds, fairy terns, sooty terns, bridled terns, wedge-tailed shearwaters and Audubon's shearwaters are all to be found during their various breeding seasons in large numbers.

Aride is also famous as the island 'where the frigates fly'. Though their nearest breeding site is Aldabra, 1,300 kilometres distant, hundreds sometimes thousands of great frigatebird and a few score lesser frigatebird reside on the northern cliffs of Aride outside their breeding season. This is the most spectacular avian sight in the granitic islands.

Among the land birds, pride of place must go to the Seychelles warbler. In 1988, twenty-nine birds were transferred from their last refuge, Cousin. Within two days, a pair built a nest and within a year the population doubled to fifty-eight. Today, there are over 300 birds and the bird has been taken off the Red Data List of Endangered Species as a result of this, the world's most dramatically successful island translocation project.

Yet the regeneration of the natural woodland during the custodianship of RSNC has meant that nature has not always needed a helping hand. In 1992, Seychelles sunbirds returned to breed for the first time this century, followed in 1994 by the Seychelles blue pigeon which also invaded by natural means to breed for the first time in more than fifty years.

The next target on the list is one of the rarest birds on earth, the Seychelles magpie robin. A recovery programme for this, one of the world's rarest species, has been implemented. While the world's only breeding population exists on Frégate, Aride has been identified as the best site to establish a second, and birds have been transferred from Frégate. The species used to breed on Aride at one time but was wiped out by collectors and possibly by cats (now eradicated from the island).

Aside from the birds, Aride has the world's greatest density of lizards, due to the abundance of food from the huge bird colonies on the island. Toss a stone into the undergrowth and skinks will scurry in all directions, being tuned into the possibility of falling eggs or chicks, spelling the arrival of lunch.

The flora includes the recently discovered Aride peponium, unique to the island. The survival of Wright's gardenia on Aride is probably due to the rich soil. The purple-spotted white flower comes into bloom several times a year, usually in the wetter, north-west monsoon, about ten days after torrential rain when the air is filled with its fragrant perfume. After the bloom dies, an inedible green fruit the size of a lemon appears, giving the plant its local name *bwa sitron*.

Several trails lead through and across Aride. It is essential to stick to marked paths because of the enormous number of ground nesting terns and tropicbirds. The reserve's warden or one of his staff guide visitors.

Trails lead through the plantation and forest areas close to the coast, up the steep hillside to viewing points on the northern cliffs, where the exquisite views must be as they were thousands of years ago. Another trail leads across Aride to the summit of Gros La Tete and down a ridge to a point above the eastern cliffs.

Proper footpaths also line the only beach, which edges the south coast for about half a kilometre. Protected by a fascinating reef, the snorkeling and the SCUBA diving are excellent. When conservationist Sir Peter Scott visited the reef for 95 minutes in 1986 he recorded 88 different species of fish. Subsequent counts by wardens and visitors have increased that number to 250. Look out for the harmless whale shark, dolphins and hawksbill turtles. The latter nest on Aride during the north-west monsoon.

Aride is only open to visitors on Wednesdays, Thursdays and Sundays. Note that landing may be difficult, if not impossible, during the south-east monsoon, so during this season it is preferable to ascertain the situation. Put all valuables in a waterproof bag when landing on and leaving the island. Visits may be arranged through any hotel or travel agency. You may also check on landing conditions by calling the warden direct on 321 600.

8

LA DIGUE AND ITS SATELLITE ISLANDS

L a Digue is one of the most charming islands in Seychelles, because, despite a population of 2,000, it remains remarkably untouched. La Digue is where people come to enjoy a few short walks, a little swimming, sunbathing, snorkeling, a picnic or two, and simply to get away from it all. However, visitors who want to get away from the get-away-from-it-all crowd should consider renting the two-house Island Lodge on Felicité, one of La Digue's satellite islands.

Although La Digue is the third largest island in Seychelles in terms of population, it is only the fourth largest in size. Five-and-a-half kilometres long by about three-and-a-half kilometres at its widest, La Digue covers more than 10 square kilometres. The highest point is Nid D'Aigles (Eagle's Nest), 333 metres above sea level. The slopes of this hill cover much of the island, and the only real lowland is on the west coast. Discovered in 1768 by Marion Dufresne, La Digue was named after one of the ships that accompanied him on that voyage. Three years later, on 12 February 1771, the French took formal possession of the island laying a 'stone of possession' — little more than a stone cairn built over a sealed bottle containing official papers.

Early settlers shared La Digue with crocodiles, lizards and fearsome-looking but non-venomous snakes. By 1777, seven families lived on the island, eking out a living from the thick forest, which stretched from the coast to the summit of Nid D'Aigles. In 1846, when farmers and fishermen had settled on the island, La Digue, according to the writer Charles Pridham, had 'not more than two thousand arpents in cultivation, of which one

Nature's granite sculptures on La Digue

thousand four hundred and fifty-four are granted and inhabited by three hundred and fifty individuals. The island is surrounded by a reef, and landing is difficult.' Eighty-five years later, the island's population was 1,255.

Most visitors arrive by sea — although the Helicopter Seychelles shuttle service now delivers an increasing number. The island's harbour is located at La Passe, the largest settlement, on the west coast. Schooners plying between Praslin and Mahé tie up at the pier. The journey to Praslin takes half an hour and the voyage to Mahé, around three hours.

There are few motor vehicles on the island — only two taxis and a bus. Visitors travel by ox-cart, bicycle, taxi or foot — and most areas are within an hour's reach of La Passe. Number ten 'La Passe-Grand Anse' in the 'Nature Trails and Walks in Seychelles' series begins at the pier, close to the covered fish market, where local fisherman come to sell their daily catch of tuna, mackerel, red snapper ('bourzwa' in Creole) and grouper ('vyey'). From the pier, follow the main dirt road south along the coast to the 'capital' of La Passe. Three roads lead inland from this main road. Take the first one, almost opposite the end of the pier, to witness typical village life in Seychelles. Then, return to the coast road, as there are some interesting landmarks to be seen on this route.

On the left-hand side a little way along the coast road there is a traditional shop. Looking seawards, note the start of Anse La Réunion beach, three kilometres long, which runs along the western coast of the island as far as the Union Estate. Out to sea, the La Digue cross and lighthouse are visible. The cross was erected in 1931 by a Swiss priest in memory of those who died while attempting to reach the island, on which it was notoriously difficult to land. In the distance, behind these two landmarks, lie the three islands of Praslin, Curieuse and Aride.

Further along the coastal road stands the island's only hospital, the Logan Hospital, named after Sir Marston Logan, Governor of Seychelles between 1942 and 1947. It is on the seaward side of the road. Two traditional houses, one of which has a thatched roof, lie between the hospital and Choppy's Bungalows, right on the beach front. All four rooms have a private shower and verandah. Choppy's restaurant serves Creole specialities and once a week a live band or disco is laid on as evening entertainment. Excursions to neighbouring islands, fishing and glass-bottom boat trips may all be arranged, while snorkeling equipment and bicycles are for hire.

Further along the road, on the left-hand side of the road, a traditional plantation house, the Yellow House, is now part of the only hotel of note on the island, La Digue Island Lodge. The hotel, which is no more than a 10-minute walk from the pier, has 43 rooms, some air-conditioned. Two restaurants serve international and Creole cuisine, and there is a SCUBA dive centre, games room and boutique. A real attraction is the beach front swimming pool, beautifully designed so that guests can sit on stools built into the pool while enjoying a drink at the poolside bar. Windsurfing, fishing and snorkeling may all be arranged. Close to the lodge is a modern supermarket.

A rough track opposite La Digue Island Lodge takes you into the interior. Where this track meets a better defined road, turn right and then take a left up to Belle Vue, just below the summit of Nid d'Aigles. From Belle Vue, it is possible to reach the highest point on the island, but it involves a fairly vigorous scramble up a rough path. If you do, you will be rewarded with spectacular views over the sea east to Marianne, south-east to Frégate, south-west to Mahé and north-west to Praslin. Return to the west coast of the island by the same route.

Back on the coastal road, continue south and, on the left-hand side of the road, just after a supermarket, you will come to a traditional coconut crusher used for extracting coconut oil. The horizontal wooden bar is pulled by an ox, which walks around in a circle, while the oil is collected in a container at the base.

On the same side of the road, there is a left turn which leads to the entrance of the La Digue Veuve Reserve, established in 1981 by the Royal Society for Nature Conservation (RSNC) to protect the beautiful Seychelles black paradise flycatcher, which breeds only on La Digue. Originally, the land on which the 15-hectare reserve stands was leased from Rene Payet. The government acquired the land after her death and the reserve is now managed by the Environment Division. It is thought to shelter five or six pairs of the endangered flycatcher — of which there are less than 50 pairs in the whole world. The male and female flycatchers are quite different in appearance: the male is completely black, with long tail streamers, hence its Creole name *vev* (in French, *veuve*) which means widow. The female bird has a black head, orange-brown wings, back and tail and a whitish underparts, as well as a short tail. Seychelles bulbuls and sunbirds are also seen regularly in the reserve.

Back on the main coastal road is La Digue Island School, for children between six and 15 years of age and next to it is the largest church on the island, dedicated to St Mary. The Paradise Fly-catcher, a self-catering establishment, also on the inland side of the road, has four two-roomed chalets, each with their own private bathroom and verandah. Its proximity to the supermarket and La Digue Island Lodge, where non-residents are welcome, is an advantage.

A large concrete cross, erected in 1931, like the one out to sea, stands at the next fork in the road. Take the right-hand fork and the road finally reaches the old, thatched colonial plantation house of Union Estate. The house, where scenes from one of the Emmanuelle films were shot, is open to the public. Just behind the house, a walled enclosure houses a number of giant tortoises. The estate grows vanilla and coconuts commercially and it is sometimes possible to see one of the 15 workers shelling coconuts to produce copra. Copra is valued for its coconut oil.

There are some quite amazing rock formations — for which La Digue is well-known — beyond the estate, as well as some idyllic coves: Pointe Source D'Argent, Anse Pierrot, Anse aux Cedres and Anse Bonnet Carre, where it is possible to sunbathe, swim, snorkel or picnic.

Returning to the concrete cross at L'Union, take the left turn and travel through the middle of the coconut plantation — to the left, old trees, to the right, new ones — belonging to the Union Estate. Further inland, on the left, the coconut plantation has been cleared for farming. Ahead rises the wooded central ridge of La Digue, on which there are several houses.

Further inland, the land surrounding the road becomes a full-blown marsh, known as 'La Mare Soupape'. Soon after the marsh, the road bends to the left. Bamboo grows close to a right-hand bend, after which there is drained marshland used for grazing cattle, and a T-junction. Turn right, with the Grand Anse River on the left-hand side running almost parallel to the road.

About 50 metres from the T-junction, an old plantation house, built in typical 19th-century style, is set back from the road. This rough track rises to some height before descending, under the shade of takamaka and Indian almond trees, to Grand Anse. Stunningly attractive, the beach is dangerous for swimming, particularly during the south-east monsoon (May to October) when there are strong undercurrents. Quite spectacular rock formations stand at either end of the beach.

A path behind the beach leads past a marshy area, to neighbouring Petite Anse, before continuing, in a north-easterly direction, to Anse Cocos. Both these beaches, although secluded and picturesque are dangerous for swimmers, especially during the south-easterlies. From Anse Cocos, the path leads across a promontory to the open beach of Anse Caiman on the east coast of the island, which is battered by the powerful waves that sweep in across thousands of kilometres of ocean. From Anse Caiman, it is a long hike to the northern tip of La Digue and back along the west coast to La Passe. The trail clings to the wild, re-mote east coast, passing the more protected shores of Anse Fourmis, Anse Banane, Anse Grosse Roche and the very long Anse Gaulettes, all of which — on calm days — are ideal destina-tions for picnickers and sunbathers. Anse Patates, the northernmost beach on the island, is unprotected by a reef and pounded by large waves.

From Anse Patates, the trail heads south along the west coast. Patatran Village is located at the northern end of the stunning Anse Sévère. The small hotel, only a two-minute walk from the Patatran Restaurant, consists of seven well-furnished chalets, each with their own private verandah. It is an ideal place to re-lax, for it is far from the main centre of island activity in La Passe. After Anse Sévère, the route cuts across the back of Pointe

Left: Ox-cart plods its way through a shady road. Right: Old grave on La Digue

Cap Barbi promontory. On the left-hand side, is the island's cemetery. About 500 metres further on, the trail reaches the pier at La Passe.

Felicité

Just over three kilometres from the north-east coast of La Digue, lies Felicité. Over two-and-a-half kilometres long by one-and-a-half kilometres wide, the island covers two-and-a-half square kilometres of granite cloaked in lush vegetation. The whole island is dominated by a hill that rises 231 metres above sea level.

With a permanent population of just 12, most of whom earn a meagre living from fishing and the island's coconut plantation, not a great deal happens on Felicité. However, some small tracks lead from the north coast to vantage points on the west coast and through the forest to the top of the hill.

It is possible to stay overnight on Felicité. La Digue Island Lodge operates Felicité Island Lodge which consists of two two-bedroomed houses built close to the beach in a traditional plantation environment. Ideally, both houses are rented by a family or friends so that they have the run of the whole island, which has a full range of watersports equipment, including a motor cruiser for big-game fishing.

Additional Information

La Digue Veuve Reserve
La Digue
No telephone
24 hours, daily
Visitor Centre
9am to 12 noon and 1pm to 4pm
Monday to Saturday

9
OTHER ISLANDS

B ird and Denis share many similar physical characteristics as they are both flat, coral islands. But while Bird is renowned, not surprisingly, for its huge bird population, Denis has become rather better known for the excellent big-game fishing off its shores. Desroches, one of the islands in the Amirantes Group, is famous for its excellent SCUBA diving opportunities.

The islands of Aldabra are something of an institution amongst international conservationists. The atoll is unlike anywhere else on earth, and a haven for several endangered species. It is possible to charter planes from Mahé to Assumption, 27 kilometres south of Aldabra.

Bird

Coral Bird Island, 0.75 kilometres wide by 1.5 kilometres long, covers just one square kilometre of land, right on the edge of the submerged plateau of the Seychelles Bank, 105 kilometres northwest of Mahé. There are few early accounts of Bird Island, as it had little to offer 18th-century explorers in search of fresh provisions. One of the first descriptions was written in 1771. It mentions a great swathe of sand, which was six miles wide. A massive sand spit still exists on the northern tip of the island, created by sand being swept up from the western coast and deposited on the tip. Sixteen years later, Malavois reported that the island had poor timber and a pond full of foul-tasting water. He also mentioned a profusion of dugongs or sea cows (now extinct), which gave the island its first name, 'Île aux Vaches Marines' — Island of Sea Cows.

The seasonal presence of huge numbers of birds resulted in the island being re-named Bird Island. Hundreds of thousands of sooty terns are found there between April and October every year. Their presence over centuries made the land rich in guano, which was extracted from the island from 1895. By 1906, however, the island's deposits were exhausted.

Interest switched to the sooty terns' eggs, considered a great delicacy in Seychelles. Every year, collectors would arrive in their boats to plunder the nests. In 1907, 100,000 eggs were removed from the island. Such massive exploitation, along with the planting of coconuts and papaya trees, affected the bird colonies. In the 1930s, 65,000 pairs bred there. Twenty years later there were just 18,000.

In 1967, a Seychellois family by the name of Savy bought Bird Island with the intention of building a small hotel on it where guests could retreat from the stresses of the outside world and bird watch. Work began in 1971, coinciding with the opening of Seychelles Airport, and soon Bird Island Lodge was ready. In the past two years, new chalets have replaced the original ones.

Several trails lead from the lodge to points on the island. The trail that heads north is of most interest, particularly between

Denis Island sets its clocks one hour ahead of the other Seychelles Islands

May and October, when up to one million sooty terns nest in the area. Other birds that may be seen include crested and fairy terns, lesser and common noddies, and a host of unusual migrants, such as broad-billed sandpipers, corncrakes and Jacobin cuckoos. It is also possible to walk the whole way around the island on the beach.

The safest swimming on Bird is off the beach in front of the lodge. Check with the staff, however, if you consider swimming elsewhere, as strong currents affect parts of the coastline, particularly those at the northern and southern tips of the island. The lodge provides facilities for a whole range of watersports, including big-game fishing.

Talk of Bird would be incomplete without mention of Esmeralda, a rather large and, despite its name, male giant tortoise, which earned a place in the Guinness Book of Records as the largest and heaviest tortoise in the world, when he weighed in at 304 kilos. Bird Island is a 30-minute flight away from Mahé. Travelling by sea takes roughly eight hours.

Denis

Almost two kilometres long by a little under one-and-a-half kilometres wide, Denis covers about one-and-a-half square kilometres. The island is 95 kilometres north of Mahé and, like Bird, is primarily flat, as it is also composed of coral.

Denis was named after the Frenchman Denis de Trobriand, who landed on the island in 1773 to bury a bottle containing the Act of Possession and claim the island in the name of the King of France. At that time, the island was covered in a profusion of birds, giant tortoises and the now extinct dugongs (sea cows).

Just over 200 years later, in 1976, another Frenchman, industrialist Pierre Burkhardt, arrived on Denis to claim the island for himself. Sick and tired of the stress associated with running his business empire, he opted for an easier life and bought Denis, beating the Shah of Iran to it by a matter of days. He then set about building the small landing strip and a hotel of 25 thatched bungalows, so that others would be able to enjoy this little slice of paradise.

From the main buildings of the hotel, a trail known as the 'Champs Elysées' leads north-east, parallel to the coast, past a small cemetery, an informal and ecumenical chapel, and the staff quarters, to the landing strip. Cross the landing strip, keep close to the northern coast and you find yourself in the island's old village, where the island's 50-odd inhabitants, most of whom work on Denis's farm and coconut plantation, live. You may be able to watch copra production. In the village you are also likely to encounter one of the giant tortoises that roam freely on the island.

Just beyond the village is the island's lighthouse, built in 1910. The lighthouse is not much more than a spindly metal frame, but it does afford panoramic views over Denis and out to sea. The path cuts through dense palm groves that cloak much of the island and thrive on the deep, fertile deposits of guano (bird droppings) accumulated over hundreds of years. Eventually, you reach the other end of the airstrip. Continue along the well-marked path, through more vegetation of the same kind — keeping a keen eye open for cobwebs — and after about 45 minutes, you should find yourself back at the hotel. The whole trail should take no more than two hours to complete. If the tide is low, it is possible to walk around much of the island on the beach. The beach route leads to some fascinating coral formations on the south-west coast, known as 'Les Caves'.

Many visit Denis as much for the sea around it as for the peace and serenity of being on a small, exclusive island. The reason why is clear — it is a Mecca for big-game fishing enthusiasts. At least five times, the waters off Denis have yielded world record dog-tooth tuna. May, October, November and December are the months to visit Denis for marlin. The rest of the year barracuda, bonito and sailfish abound. The reason for the excellent fishing conditions is the fact that Denis is situated at the edge of the submerged plateau of the Seychelles Bank, where the ocean plunges deeply. There are also opportunities for other watersports, including swimming, windsurfing and snorkeling.

An odd feature of Denis is the time — one hour ahead of the other 114 islands in Seychelles — simply so that guests may enjoy an extra hour of daylight.

Denis is served by Air Seychelles and Helicopter Seychelles charter flights. The flight from Mahé to Denis takes around 40 minutes. By sea it is approximately eight hours.

Desroches

Desroches, a platform reef 230 kilometres south-west of Mahé, is five kilometres long and about one kilometre at its widest. It covers almost four square kilometres.

The island is part of the Amirantes Group ('islands of the Admiral'), which were named in honour of Vasco da Gama in 1502.

The first recorded information on the Amirantes is dated 1609, however, when Captain Alexander Sharpeigh, on a British East India Company voyage to Aden and Surat, noted nine uninhabited islands with huge flocks of doves. The bank to which the Amirantes are attached was charted by the French in 1770 and the British in 1821–22. During the second half of the 19th century and throughout this century, these flat coral islands have prospered thanks to their extensive coconut and timber plantations, most of which are now managed by the parastatal Island Development Company.

Only four of the 25 islands that comprise the Amirantes are inhabited. They are D'Arros, Desroches, Marie Louise and Poivre. Desroches is the only one served by air. The others are visited every two or three months by supply ships.

Desroches, named after an 18th-century governor general of Mauritius, is so remote that when you fly in you could almost imagine you were landing on another planet. Desroches Island Lodge, which stretches along a fine beach, is the only hotel on the island. It has 20 spacious elegantly appointed chalets, each with its own luxurious bathroom. The chalets, ten either side of the central restaurant (serving international and Creole cuisine), bar and lounge area, are connected by palm-thatched walkways.

From the Lodge, a pleasant woodland walk runs parallel to the north-western coast, past several well-marked snorkeling points, to the village, which is about two kilometres distant. The village is home to the 40 or so plantation workers who produce copra in the traditional Seychellois manner, as well as the fresh meat and vegetables used at the hotel. The copra shed, which dominates the beach, is the most striking building in the village. Its timbers have been bleached a silver-grey by the tropical sun and its upper balcony closely resembles a ship's bridge. Nearby is the copra mill, built in 1928 by 'B.M.'. The copra was placed in the large bowl in the middle of the mill floor. A huge wooden pestle was then harnessed to an ox, which plodded around the circular mill, causing the pestle to press the copra against the bowl to extract the oil. A large cross, a memorial to some worker remembered today only by his or her initials and the date, 1953, stands close to the beach. Beyond it is the calorifier, or kiln, where the white flesh of the coconut is dried, producing the distinctive smell that pervades the atmosphere. Another building of interest is what used to be the octagonal lock-up, with its barred windows, which housed an unruly worker on odd occasions but is now an office. From the village, the path continues along the coast, reaching the northernmost tip of the island, before turning south to return to the Lodge through the interior.

Those not interested in walking may wish to indulge in some watersports. These are water-skiing, Hobie Cat sailing, para-sailing, windsurfing, canoeing, snorkeling, SCUBA diving and big-game fishing. The best season for diving is during the north-west monsoon when calm seas make it possible to visit the fantastic submerged outer rim of the lagoon. There, a wall of coral plummets thousands of metres into the depths of the Indian Ocean, a true underwater paradise. Even during the south-easterlies, however, there are plenty of other dive sites to visit. Madras snapper, moray eels, groupers and butterfly fish, to name but a few species, inhabit the shallows of the well-sheltered north-western lagoon.

Big-game fishing is also worth a whirl in the relatively unfished waters surrounding Desroches where Seychelles records have been set in the dog-tooth tuna, wahoo, rainbow runner and yellowfin tuna categories. Other game fish waiting to be hunted include sailfish and sharks. Tennis and golf facilities are expected to be developed.

While in Seychelles be free and mobile with a phone card

Cable & Wireless Seychelles Ltd

Hawksbill turtle

Desroches Island from the air

Elsewhere in the Amirantes, of particular interest are tiny Boudeuse and Etoile, both bird reserves, and Desnoeufs, home to the largest sooty tern colony in Seychelles, which should be visited between May and July when it is a fluttering mass of birds. The island has been made a protected breeding ground by local conservation authorities. A day trip to Poivre Atoll, named after Pierre Poivre who brought spices to Seychelles in the 18th century, is another popular charter choice.

Air Seychelles flies to Desroches, which is a one-hour flight from Mahé, three times a week. Charter boats to other islands can be arranged through the Marine Charter Association.

Aldabra

Aldabra, the second of Seychelles' two World Heritage Sites, lies 1,150 kilometres south-west of Mahé and covers 154 square kilometres, roughly one-third of Seychelles' terrestrial territory. It is the world's largest raised coral atoll.

It is possible that Arab sailors trading between Zanzibar and the Comoros may have known of this group of islands as early as the Middle Ages, for Aldabra could be a corruption of Al-khadra, the Arabic word for 'the green'. The Portuguese may have sighted the islands at the beginning of the 16th century, because Aldabra appeared on one of their maps in 1511. However, the forbidding coastline, lack of fresh water and its distance from the main shipping routes meant that it remained without human presence for a long time.

In the 19th century, Aldabra began to be exploited by seamen for its tortoises, which provided an excellent source of fresh meat on long journeys. In 1874, a group of scientists including Charles Darwin appealed to the government of Mauritius (under whose jurisdiction Aldabra came) to take measures to safeguard the giant tortoise. The Mauritian Government reacted initially by banning a woodcutting project that was worrying the scientists; then, in 1891, it banned the taking of tortoises, while still allowing turtles to be caught. The slaughter of green turtles therefore continued unabated until 1945. Nineteen years later, Great Britain and the United States developed a plan to establish a military base on either Aldabra, Desroches, Farquhar or Diego Garcia. The wrath of British ecologists was aroused and, in the end, only Diego Garcia was turned into an airbase. In 1971 a Research Station was established on Aldabra by the Royal Society, which handed over its responsibilities to the Seychelles Islands Foundation, when it was set up in 1979. In 1981, it became a Special Reserve under the Seychelles National Parks and Nature Conservancy Act, culminating with its UNESCO designation as a World Heritage Site in 1982.

Today, less than 20 people live on Aldabra, working on the research station that has been constructed on Picard, one of the four main islands. The other three islands of note are Polymnie, Malabar and Grande Terre. A cross-section of the islands would reveal a mysterious, mushroom-shaped outline akin to the cloud structure caused by an exploding H-bomb. These strange silhouettes have been caused by marine erosion, for water from the huge lagoon rushes between the islands when the tide goes out and then sweeps back past them with the incoming tide. The strange shape of the islands creates an almost impenetrable shoreline. Meanwhile the rough limestone surface of these islands makes them pretty much inhospitable to man.

This island group is home to 150,000 tortoises, the world's largest population, and Aldabra has the honour of being the only place in Seychelles (and one of only two places in the world, the other being the Galapagos) where the giant tortoise lives in its natural state. The average age of these tortoises is believed to be about 60 to 70 years and the average weight around 50 kilos. The tortoises feed on turf, sedges and shrubs, using a friend as a step ladder to reach the top leaves.

Unfortunately, the green turtle has not fared as well as the giant tortoise, but it has survived. About 2,400 breeding female green turtles nest each year on Aldabra, 50 per cent of the total Seychelles population. That is a fraction of the figure that existed at the turn of the century, but there are signs that the population is increasing. The continued survival of both the green turtle and the giant tortoise in Aldabra has, undoubtedly, been helped by UNESCO proclaiming the island a World Heritage Site.

Aside from the tortoise and the turtle, Aldabra boasts some interesting birdlife. Two full species of bird — the white-throated rail and the Aldabran drongo — are endemic to the group. And there are more varieties of breeding seabirds than on any other island in Seychelles.

Aldabra is also home to 176 species of flowering plant, 19 of which are endemic and 22 of which are shared with neighbouring islands. Of these, the Aldabra lily is the most remarkable.

Charter planes fly to the airstrip on Assumption, one of the islands in the Aldabra Group which is some 27 kilometres from Aldabra itself. From there, it is a three-hour boat ride to Aldabra.

Greater flamingos over Aldabra

Seychelles blue pigeon

Mushroom-shaped coral bank formed by constant erosion

Seychelles Fact File

Accommodation

Seychelles offers a wide variety of hotels, as well as smaller guest-houses and self catering accommodation. Lodges with bungalows as rooms are normal on smaller islands such as Denis and Bird. Camping is not allowed anywhere in Seychelles.

Although some tour operators and guide books give hotels a star standard, there is as yet no star grading system in Seychelles and many hotels do not match the high standards found elsewhere in the world. In fact, it is not uncommon for visitors to talk of Seychelles as 'a five-star destination, with three-star service'. In general, rooms are little more than basic and the service slow.

The largest hotel on Mahé, with around 200 rooms, is The Plantation Club Hotel, closely followed by the Beau Vallon Bay Hotel, the Mahé Beach Hotel and the Reef Golf Club Hotel, all with more than 150 rooms. The Northolme and Sunset Beach Hotels are smaller, but among the better units on the island.

Most hotels have boutiques and watersports facilities.

Banks

The following banks operate in the capital, Victoria, and buy and sell foreign currencies in the form of drafts, travellers cheques and notes.

Barclays Bank
Bank of Baroda
Habib Bank
Banque Française Commerciale
Nouvobanq (Seychelles International)

Camera Equipment

Given the outstanding beauty of the landscape and seascape, as well as the colourful characters of the Seychellois, it is difficult to take a bad picture of Seychelles. On the other hand, sparkling white sand beaches, multi-hued seas of green and blue, as well as cloudless azure skies play havoc with exposure settings, particularly when contrasted with lush foliage or dark skins. To ensure imbalances are corrected consider using a polarising filter, which reduces the flare caused by bright sunshine and brilliant colours.

Photo Eden, in Victoria and Mont Fleuri, and Kim Koon, also in the capital, offer one-hour film processing services. It is also possible to purchase camera equipment in these shops.

Do not leave your camera exposed to the sun, especially around noon. Too many tales of cameras melting when left on the front dashboard of a car are told. A few minutes of midday heat may also fog your film.

The Seychellois rarely object to having their photograph taken but: always ask first.

Chemists

The only chemists in Seychelles are in Victoria. Government health clinics in many villages, however, may be able to provide emergency prescriptions.

The Central Pharmacy at Victoria Hospital is open Monday to Friday from 0800 to 1800 and on Saturdays and Sundays from 0800 to 1200. Tel: 224 400

Behram's Pharmacy in Victoria House, Victoria is open Monday to Friday from 0815 to 1715, closing for lunch between 1300 and 1400, and on Saturdays from 0800 to 1230. Tel: 225 559

Fock Heng's Pharmacy in Revolution Avenue, Victoria is open Monday to Friday from 0830 to 1700 and on Saturdays from 0830 to 1230. Tel: 322 751

Climate

Seychelles experiences a monsoon climate. The south-east monsoon blows between May and October and the north-west monsoon blows between November and April. In general, however, Seychelles experiences a humid tropical climate with little variation in temperature (between 24°Celsius and 30°Celsius).

May to October is known as the 'Dry Season'. Traditionally,

Maki

rainfall is particularly low during June and July and, apart from early May and late October, thundery weather and heavy downpours are rare. If there is any precipitation, it is mostly light and short. However, the monsoon winds increase in strength and constancy during this period, reaching their peak towards late July and early August. Wind speeds may touch 40 kilometres an hour, with gusts of up to 100 kilometres an hour. May is still relatively warm, with average daily temperatures of around 28°Celsius, but moving into June, July and August, temperatures fall as the cool south-easterly breeze establishes itself. Temperatures are at their lowest towards late July and early August — at the peak of the southern hemisphere winter. Average temperatures for June through to October are in the vicinity of 26°Celsius. May and June are traditionally the sunniest months of the year with sunshine duration averaging eight hours.

November to April constitutes what the Seychellois call the 'Rainy Season' as it's often wet and humid with occasional thunderstorms. January is usually the wettest month with average rainfall of 379.4 millimetres. During this period rain may fall at any time of day or night, but most often in the afternoon. It's not uncommon to experience two or three consecutive days of heavy rain. This period can be hot too, but the heat is often kept in check by the cooling effect of the abundant clouds and rain. Average temperatures range from 26.8°Celsius in November to 28°Celsius in April, traditionally the warmest month. With a high percentage of cloud cover, the hours of sunshine are often as little as five hours a day.

Compared with the south-east monsoons, the north-westerlies are light. Average speeds range from 10 to 13 kilometres, resulting in calm sea conditions. On odd occasions, however, strong winds may be experienced for short periods of two or three days, in association with minor disturbances over the area or the development of cyclones to the south. During this period, speeds of over 30 kilometres an hour and gusts in excess of 70 kilometres per hour may be experienced, leading to rough sea conditions in Seychelles waters.

There is no set tourist season when it is better to visit Seychelles, but the south-east monsoon (May to October) usually produces the longest hours of sunshine, slightly cooler temperatures and lower humidity. These conditions, however, are not invariable.

Visitors with a particular interest should take note of the following suggestions: those interested in walking should travel to Seychelles during the cooler, drier south-east monsoon; those who wish to dive should travel between the two monsoons i.e. April–May or October–November when the sea is calmer and visibility higher; ornithologists travel during the south-east monsoon, particularly in April when the new breeding season begins, and October which is good for migrants.

A weather forecast may be obtained by telephoning the Meterological Office on tel: 373 377, but the weather is so variable in Seychelles that islanders joke that weather reports only tell what has occurred the day before. It is often easier, and more accurate, to look out of the window to check the weather.

Communications

Post

The Central Post Office (Tel: 225 222) is in Victoria, close to the Clock Tower, and opens Monday to Friday from 0800 to 1600 and on Saturdays from 0800 to 1200. Otherwise, stamps may be bought from many shops throughout the islands and most hotel boutiques. Hotels will mail letters and postcards, and post boxes are located in police stations in various villages around the islands.

The Central Post Office has a Philatelic Bureau for collectors who wish to buy or place orders for special issues and first-day covers.

Telephones, Facsimilies, Telexes and Cables

Seychelles has an efficient communications service. Telephone calls are fairly expensive both within Seychelles and internationally, however — rates are published in the telephone directory.

Direct dialling is available to most countries around the world and directories providing international codes and information

Auberge Louis XVII

HOTEL AND RESTAURANT

PO BOX 104, LA LOUISE, SEYCHELLES
TEL: 344411/344404; FAX: 344428

The Auberge is named after Louis XVII, who is reputed to have escaped to Seychelles during the French revolution of 1789. Now a delightful retreat for holiday makers, the hotel is set in ten acres of private grounds. Despite its seclusion, it is conveniently situated halfway between Victoria and Seychelles International Airport, only three kilometres from the centre of Victoria, with a magnificent panoramic view of the capital, the nearby islands and the St Anne Marine National Park.

A popular feature of the hotel is its gourmet restaurant, which serves a vast selection of mouthwatering dishes, and caters for fast business lunches as well as leisurely meals for visitors. Specialities include Bouillabaisse prepared with freshly caught seafood, a wide variety of fresh pasta dishes, Bourgeois grilled with ginger, and king prawns in a white wine sauce. The restaurant also offers a splendid selection of top-quality steaks, vegetarian dishes and irresistible desserts.

Miles from home....
but not out of reach

Barclays Bank PLC provides a complete banking service.

Located at Independence Avenue, Victoria, Mahé
Market Street, Victoria, Mahé
Anse Boileau, Mahé
Beau Vallon, Mahé
Seychelles International Airport
Anse Reunion, La Digue
Baie Ste. Anne, Praslin
Grand Anse, Praslin

are found in many hotel rooms. Expect to pay heavy commission charges if you use the room phone.

A cheaper way to phone is through Cable and Wireless, in Victoria's Francis Rachel Street, which provides a 24-hour international service for telephone, telex, telegram and facsimile communications.

Public call boxes — both coin and card — are dotted throughout the islands. Cards are in units of SR30, SR60, SR100 (120 units) and SR200 (240 units). Phone cards may be bought from several outlets throughout Seychelles including Cable and Wireless and the airports on both Mahé and Praslin.

To make an overseas call from a private phone, dial 0, followed by the country code, the area code and the number required. If you encounter any problems, dial 151 for international enquiries.

All numbers in Seychelles in 1994 had six numbers. In cases of difficulty, dial 181 for local directory enquiries.

All telephone operators speak English.

The international code for Seychelles is 248. The following direct dialling codes may be of use from Seychelles: United Kingdom (044), USA & Canada (01) and Australia (061).

Currency and Credit Cards

There is no limit on the amount of foreign currency brought into the country in the form of travellers cheques, bankers drafts or letters of credit. However, it is illegal to export more than SR100 in notes and more than SR10 in coins. All excess money must be exchanged before leaving.

The Seychelles currency is the Seychelles Rupee, which is issued by the Central Bank of Seychelles in the following denominations: notes - SR100, SR50, SR25, SR10; coins - SR5 and SR1. The rupee is divided into 100 cents and the following cent coins are issued: 25c, 10c and 5c.

Major credit cards such as American Express, Diners Club, Visa and Master Card are accepted by most hotels, but not widely used by shops and restaurants. Check beforehand, if in doubt.

Customs Regulations

A reasonable volume of personal effects, such as cameras and film, can be freely imported. Banned imports include any type of firearm (including air pistols, rifles and spearguns), animals, agricultural and horticultural produce.

Visitors are restricted to duty-free items of 200 cigarettes or fifty cigars, one litre of wine or spirits and one small bottle of perfume, together with other dutiable articles up to a value of 1,000 rupees (approximately £120 sterling).

No departure tax is levied on visitors leaving Seychelles.

Electricity

Electricity is 240 volts AC 50Hz with three point, square-pin plugs. Adaptors are provided by most hotels. On outer islands such as La Digue, where the roads are little more than rough tracks and there is no street lighting, it may be useful to carry a torch.

Embassies and High Commissions

Seychelles Missions Abroad

UNITED KINGDOM
Mr Silvester Radegonde
111 Baker Street
2nd Floor, Eros House
London W1M 1FG
Tel: (071) 224 1660
Telex: 28146 SEYCOM C
Fax: (071) 487 5756

UNITED STATES AND CANADA
Mr Mark Marengo
820 Second Avenue
Suite 927F
New York

Seychelles...

One hundred sunkissed islands a thousand miles
from anywhere in the heart of the Indian Ocean.
White sands... turquoise waters... tropical forests...
granite mountains... exotic flora and fauna.
These are the islands of your dreams.

*...out of this world,
but not out of
your reach.*

*See your travel agent,
or send for your
free brochure.*

chelles
A THOUSAND MILES

New York 10017
Tel: (212) 687 9766
Telex: 220032 FMUNUR
Fax: (212) 808 4975

AUSTRALIA
Mr Guy Robert
Honorary Consul General
271 Canning Road
Les Murdie
Perth
WA 6076
Tel: 291 6570

Mr John Charody
Honorary Consul General
6th Floor
55 Macquaire Street
Sydney
NSW 2000
Tel: 231 4802

Foreign Diplomatic Missions in Seychelles
AMERICAN EMBASSY
Victoria House
PO Box 251
Victoria
Tel: 225 256
Fax: 225 189

BRITISH HIGH COMMISSION
Victoria House
PO Box 161
Victoria
Tel: 225 225
Fax: 225 127

Emergencies

If, in the case of an emergency, the Police, Fire Brigade or an Ambulance are required, dial 999 and ask for the necessary service.

In cases of non-emergencies, the following telephone numbers may be of use:

Police

Central   322 011
Mont Fleuri   322 011
Beau Vallon   247 242
Anse Royale   371 226
Praslin   233 251
La Digue   234 251

Hospitals

Central Hospital 224 400
Anse Royale   371 222
Praslin   233 333
La Digue   234 255

Facilities for the Disabled

Seychelles International Airport, cruiseships operating in Seychelles waters and tour buses cater for the disabled. Wheel chairs, for example, are on hand at the airport. However, excursions by boat are not designed to accommodate the disabled. Ideally, travel agents, tour operators and hotels should be given advance notice of a disabled visitor, so that special arrangements may be made.

Festivals and Local Events

The Creole Festival takes place in late October or early November. The Creole Institute, National Theatre, National Museum and National Heritage organise a series of concerts, dance shows, poem recitals and exhibitions.

In June, there is a one-day Music Festival when both traditional

Allamanda Hotel

*Where little things
mean a lot...
and big things
mean a beach all to
yourself.*

Anse Forbans is one of the world's great
beaches — and it's all yours, with only
nine other couples.

The Allamanda Hotel provides a
personal, unparalleled service for guests.

Step out of your airconditioned, en-
suite bedroom down to our beach
restaurant and bar. Enjoy the intimate
atmosphere of this colonial-style hotel.
Relax in huge wicker chairs in our spacious
lounge, sipping a tropical cocktail. Sample
our mouthwatering cuisine,
including tiger prawns in
garlic butter or any of the
other Creole specialities
(the fishing boat calls daily
with its morning catch).

We're ideal for
honeymooners and
romantics of any age — we
can even arrange your
wedding for you!

Anse Forbans
PO Box 378
Mahé,
Seychelles
Tel: 366266;
Fax: 366175

A BETTER VIEW OF PARADISE

ISLAND TRANSFERS AND SCENIC FLIGHTS

and modern bands, including the National Orchestra, perform in every corner of the island.

Ask at the Tourist Information Office in Victoria's Independence House for details of any other local festivals, or check in *Seychelles Rendezvous*, the free tourist magazine published by the Department of Tourism and Transport. Check with Emmanuel D'Offay at the National Arts Council on tel: 225 477 if you are interested in viewing the national art exhibitions that are staged from time to time.

Illness and Injury

There is a well-equipped Central Hospital in Victoria and smaller hospitals or clinics at Anse aux Pins, Anse Boileau, Anse Royale, Baie Lazare, Beau Vallon, Beolière, Corgat Estate, English River, Glacis, Les Mamelles, Mont Fleuri, North Point, Port Glaud and Takamaka in Mahé; Baie St Anne and Grande Anse in Praslin; La Digue and Silhouette. Most doctors speak English and visitors may obtain medical treatment at charges based on the actual cost of the service provided. Some larger clinics also offer dental and physiotherapy services. In addition, a few hotels have duty nurses.

The clinics are open Monday to Friday between 0730 and 1700 and on Saturdays from 0730 to 1200. Emergency treatment may be obtained at the Central Hospital at all times.

For a list of private practices, consult the yellow pages of the local telephone directory.

Language

Kreol (Creole) is the official language in Seychelles. However, many of the locals also speak French and English, the latter being the language of the law and commerce.

Newspapers published in Seychelles include *Seychelles Nation*, a trilingual morning paper published by the government's Central Information Services Division from Monday to Saturday. Also *Seychelles Independent* and *Regar*, independent trilingual (mainly English) weekly papers. The international coverage in both these newspapers is limited.

A radio service is provided by the Seychelles Broadcasting Corporation (SBC) which broadcasts on 219 metres 1368kHz from 0600 to 1330 and from 1500 to 2200 Monday to Friday and from 0600 to 2200 on Saturdays and Sundays. The English news bulletin can be heard at 1900. The Far East Broadcasting Association (FEBA) transmits religious radio programmes throughout the Far East, Asia and some Arab countries. The BBC World Service may be received on various frequencies.

SBC also provides the country's television service, which broadcasts from 1745 to 2230 Monday to Friday, 1500 to 2300 on Saturdays and from 1400 to 2300 on Sundays in three languages — Creole, French and English. The English news headlines are at 1800.

Legal Advice

Visitors to Seychelles who are arrested should contact the relevant diplomatic mission. However, should this prove impossible, lawyers may be contacted at either the Law Centre, located in Victoria's Kingsgate House, or at the Supreme Court or in the yellow pages of the local telephone directory. In Seychelles, lawyers are either solicitors or barristers, or both, as the law allows for a fused profession. They are required by law to be professionally qualified, enrolled and admitted by the local Supreme Court and licensed by the Seychelles Licensing Authority. Most have qualified in Great Britain and other Commonwealth countries.

In Seychelles, the Civil Law is based on the French Napoleonic Code, which has been adapted to modern life in Seychelles and is now known as the Civil Code of Seychelles. Criminal law is based on English laws, but has also been adapted for use in Seychelles.

Law is mostly applied in courts and tribunals, the main courts being the Magistrate Court, the Supreme Court and the Court of Appeal (the higest court in the land). The administration of the courts is centred on the Registrar of the Supreme Court in

Age-old

traditions

of banking

combine

with a modern

forward-looking

approach

to help us

spread our wings

in Seychelles and

in the region

Experience the best of Seychelles

Berjaya Beau Vallon Bay Beach Resort & Casino,
For reservations contact:
Telephone: (248) 247141; Telefax: (248) 247943

Berjaya Mahé Beach Resort & Casino,
For reservations contact:
Telephone: (248) 378451; Telefax: (248) 378517

Berjaya Praslin Beach Resort
For reservations contact:
Telephone: (248) 232222; Telefax: (248) 232244

Victoria. The principal legal adviser of the government is the attorney-general, who is also directly responsible for all criminal prosecutions.

Maps

Detailed ordnance survey maps, at a cost of SR20 each, are available from the survey office on the ground floor of Independence House in Victoria. The office is located at the far end of the building's 5th June Avenue face. Less detailed maps may be obtained from the Tourist Information Centre, also on the ground floor of Independence House.

Measurements

The metric system is used in Seychelles. Conversions are:
1 kilogram (1,000 grams) = 2.2lb
1 litre = 1.75 pints
4.5 litres = 1 gallon
8 km = 5 miles

National Holidays

Official
New Year's Day: 1 and 2 January
Labour Day: 1 May
Constitution Day : 18 June
Independence Day: 29 June

Religious
Good Friday: March or April
Corpus Christi: June
Assumption (La Digue festival): 15 August
All Saints Day: 1 November
Immaculate Conception: 8 December
Christmas Day: 25 December

Passports and Visas

All visitors must have a valid passport. Visas are not required for those wishing to holiday in Seychelles. On arrival visitors are granted a pass valid for one month as long as they have a valid onward or return ticket. It may be extended at three-monthly intervals for up to 12 months on production of an onward or return ticket and valid travel documents. Extensions may be obtained at the Immigration and Civil Status Division, Independence House, Independence Avenue, Victoria (PO Box 430 Tel: 225 333) Monday to Friday from 0800 to 1100 and 1300 to 1500. There is no charge for an extension of this pass.

Travellers by sea are exempt from these requirements provided that the master of the vessel, or the shipping agent, gives the immigration authorities a written guarantee of their repatriation.

Personal Insurance and Medical Cover

The islands are free of rabies, malaria and most major diseases. Vaccination certificates are not, therefore, a requirement. However, check the latest requirements with a doctor or travel agent prior to travel.

It is advisable to take out medical insurance to cover repatriation expenses, should you need to be evacuated in an emergency. Cover may be bought in Seychelles from the State Assurance Company, but it is more practical to buy it before leaving home.

Religion

The predominant religion on the islands, to which 90 per cent of the population belongs, is Roman Catholic. Other Christian denominations such as the Church of England, Seventh Day Adventists and Bahai represent another eight per cent of the population. There are Catholic and Anglican cathedrals in the capital of Victoria with parishes for every district on the principal islands. The other faiths practised in Seychelles include Bahai, Islam and Hinduism.

Shopping

There are many things to buy in Seychelles — if only they were more affordable.

Several artists — painters, potters, woodworkers, batik artists — practice on the islands and a piece of their art will always be a beautiful reminder of Seychelles. A new gallery is to open above the Pirate's Arms in Victoria where the work of a wide range of local artists will be on display. Pieces will be for sale, but for those who wish to visit the artists at their studios, a directory of artists will be available from the gallery. However the studios of most of the artists do appear in the text of this book.

Model ships may be bought from several sources including La Marine at Anse Aux Pins on the west coast of Mahé where it is possible to visit the workshops and see the ships being made.

Traditional craftworks such as woven baskets, bags, hats and items made from coconuts, as well as modern jewellery, pottery and paintings — all produced locally — are on sale at CODEVAR in Victoria's Camion Hall. Curios and knick-knacks such as keyrings of the *coco-de-mer*, T-shirts, pareos, spices and tea are sold by the stalls that line Independence Avenue close to the Clock Tower, as well as from boutiques dotted around the island, particularly in major hotels.

Shells, corals and jewellery made from turtleshell are also sold at numerous outlets, but please think twice before buying fragile goods that are unlikely to survive the journey home. Remember that turtleshell is illegal in most countries; and dead coral and shells are a poor reminder of what they once were. Seychelles reefs are being substantially damaged by the coral trade.

Clothes (particularly T-shirts and pareos) are widely available in a variety of styles and designs. Sunstroke Design Studio, which has outlets in Market Street, Victoria and close to the Beau Vallon Police Station produces some of the best local clothes.

Stamps have become a popular item for tourists to take with them when they leave Seychelles. Not surprisingly, given that they are among the most beautiful in the world, depicting as they do the unique flora and fauna of the islands. Stamps may be bought from the Philatelic Bureau, located at the Central Post Office in Victoria.

Coco-de-mer nuts — the fun-shaped fruit of the *coco-de-mer* tree which resemble human buttocks — are best bought from the Vallée de Mai in Praslin.

Women, in particular, may enjoy the unique fragrances of Kreolfleurage Parfums and a traditional wooden pestle and mortar, an integral part of the Creole cuisine, which can be bought in Victoria's market.

Shops generally open from 0800 to 1700 from Monday to Friday (some close for an hour at lunch) and from 0800 to 1200 on Saturdays. Some general stores also open on Sunday mornings.

Sports and Pastimes

Beach Guide

All beaches in Seychelles are open to the public although access via hotel entrances may be restricted. The most popular beach on Mahé for those who wish to swim in the sea is, without a doubt, Beau Vallon, which some may say has been ruined by over-crowding, but it's all relative. The rest of the beaches on Mahé are deserted, so even a handful of people constitutes a crowd on this island. If, however, Beau Vallon is too 'crowded', try Bel Ombre, which is just around the corner, on the north coast of the island.

Anse Royale on the east coast and Baie Lazare on the west coast are good beaches for snorkeling but not so much for swimming. The beaches of Grande Anse and Anse Intendance are considered dangerous for swimming, particularly during the south-east monsoon when powerful currents may be experienced.

On Praslin, the best beaches for swimming are Anse Volbert on the east coast and Anse Lazio on the north coast. Anse Kerlan in the west is considered dangerous for swimming particularly during the north-west monsoon when powerful currents flow.

On La Digue, the west side of the island where Anse Union and Anse La Réunion are located is ideal for swimming, while the beaches on the wilder, south-eastern side of the island such as Anse Cocos, Petite Anse, Grande Anse, Anse Songe and Anse

Marron are considered dangerous, especially during the southeast monsoon.

Boating and Sailing, Water and Land Sports

Seychelles Yacht Club
Victoria
Mahé
Tel: 322 362

Marine Charter Association
Box 469, Victoria
Mahé
Tel: 322 126
Fax: 224 679

Dive Centres

Marine Divers
Beau Vallon Bay Hotel
Beau Vallon, Mahé
Tel: 247 171 Ext 8133
Fax: 247 945

Mahé Beach Hotel
Diving Centre
Port Glaud, Mahé
Tel: 378 451
Fax: 378 517

Marine Divers
Northolme Hotel
Glacis, Mahé
Tel: 261 222
Fax: 247 945

Aqua Diving Services
Amitié, Praslin
Tel: 233 972
Fax: 233 015

Praslin Beach Diving Centre
Anse Volbert
Praslin
Tel: 232 222
Fax: 232 148

Waterline Pty Limited
Plantation Club Hotel
Baie Lazare, Mahé
Tel: 361 361

Seychelles Underwater
Centre
Coral Strand Hotel
Beau Vallon, Mahé
Tel: 247 357
Fax: 344 223

Marine Divers
La Digue Island Lodge
Anse La Réunion
La Digue
Tel: 234 232
Fax: 234 100

Desroches Dive Centre
Desroches Island
Tel: 229 003
Fax: 229 002

Poseidon Diving &
Water Sports
Silhouette
Tel: 224 003

Aside from watersports — water-skiing, parasailing, snorkeling, SCUBA diving, big-game fishing, sailing, charters — visitors to the islands may enjoy rock climbing, trekking, cycling, hiking, golf, tennis and horse-riding.

Tourist Information Centres

UNITED KINGDOM
Mrs Liz Lower
2nd Floor
Eros House
111 Baker Street
London W1M 1FE
Tel: (071) 224 1670
Fax: (071) 487 5756
Telex: 28146 SEYCOM

USA & CANADA
Mr Mark Marengo
820 Second Avenue
Suite 927F
New York
New York 10017
Tel: (212) 687 9766
Fax: (212) 808 4975
Telex: 220032 FMUNUR

Travel

By Air

Air Seychelles flies twice weekly to London's Gatwick Airport, one service operating via Rome, the other via Zurich. Weekly services also operate to Frankfurt, Paris, Madrid (via Nairobi) and a second service to Rome (via Bahrain). There are weekly flights to Singapore and Johannesburg. The Air Seychelles office is located in Victoria House, Victoria, tel: 225 220.

Aeroflot fly from Moscow once a week (via Larnaca and Aden), Air France flies from Paris four times a week going on to Réunion and Mauritius, and back to Paris via Seychelles, British Airways flies to Seychelles twice a week, going on to Mauritius and returning via Seychelles to London's Gatwick and Kenya Airways serves Seychelles from Nairobi twice a week.

Approximate flying times are as follows: from London (12 hours), from Singapore (seven hours), the Gulf (five hours), South Africa (4.5 hours), Nairobi (three hours) and Mauritius (2.5 hours). Flight information may be obtained from the following Air Seychelles offices:

Air Seychelles Limited
Kelvin House
Kelvin Way, Crawley
West Sussex RH10 2SE
United Kingdom
Tel: (0293) 536 313
Fax: (0293) 562 353

General Sales Agent
International Pty Limited
363 Victoria Street
Abbotsford 3067
Melbourne, Australia
Tel: (03) 429 6522
Fax: (03) 427-0379

APS Inc North America
5757 W Century Boulevard
Suite 660, Los Angeles
CA 90045-5631, USA
Tel: (310) 670 7303
Fax: (310) 338 0708

Seychelles Holidays
76/7 Elizabeth Street
Sydney NSW 2000
Australia
Tel: (02) 223 7553
Fax: (02) 221 2368

Skylink Travel Limited
593 Yonge Street
Suite 230, Toronto
Ontario, Canada M4Y 1Z4
Tel: (416) 922 0037
Fax: (416) 922 3588

Seychelles International Airport, located on the east coast of Mahé, is small and simple, with duty-free shopping for arriving and departing visitors, banks and car-hire facilities. There is a stop for buses travelling to the south of the island just outside the airport, buses travelling north to the capital of Victoria stop on the opposite side of the road from the airport. Taxis are available.

For island hopping, Air Seychelles operates scheduled inter-island flights between Mahé-Praslin and Mahé-Desroches. In addition, there are charter services to the islands of Bird, Denis and Frégate. For more information, contact Inter-island reservations in Seychelles on tel: 373 101.

By Helicopter

For visitors who wish to enjoy a bird's eye view of these idyllic islands, there is no better way than from a helicopter.

Helicopter Seychelles, established in 1992 by Vic Davies, is the only helicopter enterprise in Seychelles. The company operates charter and shuttle services to the islands of Silhouette, Denis and La Digue; transfers between outlying islands so that passengers do not have to transit in Mahé as they do if they use the services of Air Seychelles; scenic trips of Mahé and the inner islands of Seychelles from various points including its base at Seychelles International Airport and The Plantation Club Hotel 'helispot' on the west coast of Mahé; charters for film and video crews; an emergency evacuation service; and ship servicing. However, this fledgling company is expanding rapidly. For up-to-date information on services offered, contact:

Helicopter Seychelles
Seychelles International Airport
PO Box 595, Victoria, Mahé, Seychelles
Tel: 375 400
Fax: 375 277

By Bus

For those staying on the main island of Mahé who like to travel independently and enjoy a little local flavour, the Seychelles Public Transport Corporation (SPTC) operates several bus services from its Central Station in Victoria to all villages on the island. The destination of the bus is written on a placard displayed in the front window. These bus services run between 0530 and 2130. Bus services also operate on Praslin and La Digue.

By Car

There are numerous car hire companies in Seychelles. They include:

Mahé
Avis Rent-A-Car
Box 224
Victoria
Tel: 224 511

Budget Rent-A-Car
Box 72
Victoria
Tel: 344 280

Europcar International
Box 559
Victoria
Tel: 225 303

Hertz Leisure Cars
Box 600
Victoria
Tel: 322 447

Mein's Car Hire
Box 169
Victoria
Tel: 266 005
Tel: 233 555

Sunshine Cars
Box 127
Victoria
Tel: 224 671

Praslin
Austral Car Rental
Baie St Anne
Tel: 232 015

Prestige Car Hire
Grand Anse
Tel: 233 226

Standard Car Hire
Amitié

A full list of car hire companies is to be found in the yellow pages of the local telephone directory.

Emergencies

– The conditions of contract are shown on the hire vehicle documents which should be kept in the vehicle at all times. In cases of breakdown contact should be made with the hirer of the vehicle. The police should attend any accidents and the hirers of the vehicle should be informed.

Documents needed

– Drivers must be over 21 years of age and should possess a valid driving licence.

Driving conditions

– Motorists drive on the left-hand side of the road. Wearing of seatbelts is not compulsory. Speed limits are as follows: 40kph in Victoria and other 'built up' areas; 65kph on the rest of the island. On Praslin, speed is limited to 25kph. All main roads on Mahé are well-surfaced, but take care and drive slowly, especially when driving on the roads that cross over the island as there are no safety barriers at the road edges and there are many sharp corners. On Praslin, the roads are not all as well-surfaced as on Mahé, hence the lower speed limit.

Fuel

– The petrol stations on Mahé are located in Victoria's Francis Rachel Street, Anse Royale, Beau Vallon, Baie Lazare, Port Glaud and at the Airport. All close in the evening.

By Bicycle

An environmentally-aware and healthy way to travel is by bicycle. On Mahé, Hercules Bicycle Hire (tel: 373 039) rents touring and mountain bikes. They have reception desks at Le Meridien Barbarons and the Reef Golf Club Hotel. Excursions to various places of interest in the south of the island may be arranged. Bicycle is the ideal mode of transport on La Digue.

By Taxi

There are around 130 taxis on Mahe which normally wait at the International Airport Terminal when flights are due in, major hotels and the Central Taxi Station in Victoria. Fewer than 20 taxis operate on Praslin, many of which wait for the arrival of the Air Seychelles inter-island flights at the Airstrip in Amitié. Although taxis on Praslin are not, in general, stationed at major hotels, they may be contacted immediately through any Praslin hotel reception desk.

The 24-hour service offered by taxis is of a high standard, which is maintained through the supervision of the Taxi Drivers Association. Any complaints should be addressed to this official body at Box 555, Victoria, tel: 323 895, and copied to Tourism Division.

However, taxis — which are recognisable by a 'taxi' logo on their roof — may be an expensive method of transport. Although all are now fitted with a meter, passengers should insist the meter is turned on before setting off. If calling a taxi to collect you, ask for the meter to be turned on before departure. Do not believe drivers who say it will be cheaper without the meter. Note that there is a 25 to 35 per cent supplement for journeys made at night and there are extra charges for luggage.

By Excursion

Visitors who would prefer to do all their sightseeing with an experienced guide, should contact one of the three main tour operators:

Mason's Travel
Box 459
Revolution Avenue
Victoria
Mahé
Tel: 322 642

Travel Services Seychelles
Box 356
Mahé Trading Building
Victoria
Mahé
Tel: 222 414

National Travel Agency
Box 611
Kingsgate House
Victoria
Mahé
Tel: 224 900

Weddings

In order for visitors to Seychelles to be married in a civil ceremony, the following documents must be produced: passports and birth certificates, a document proving that there is no reason — legal or otherwise — why the marriage should not take place (otherwise, couples will be asked to sign an affidavit in Seychelles having made a solemn declaration to this effect) and, if one of the parties is a divorcee, widow or widower, the divorce document (decree nisi absolute) or death certificate must be produced. Couples wishing to marry should call at the Central Civil Status Office in Victoria's Independence House with all the documents. According to Seychelles law, wedding bans must be published at least 11 days before a marriage may be conducted. For a fee of SR100, a Special Licence may be obtained, which reduces this waiting period to just two days.

Those wishing to marry in a religious ceremony should contact one of the island's priests directly.

For further information, contact:

Civil Status Office

Management and Information Systems Division

PO Box 206

Independence House

Victoria

Seychelles.

Photographs by:

Mohamed Amin: 3, 7, 8, 10, 35, 59, 82, 90, 98, 102, 103, 110, 119, 131, 143, 158, 163, 166, 167.

Duncan Willetts: 18, 23, 26, 27, 30, 31, 39, 42, 46, 54, 67, 75, 79, 94, 95, 107, 114, 115, 118, 134, 135, 146, 155, 163 (top).

Debbie Gaiger: 1, 2, 14, 34, 51, 62, 70, 83, 86, 87, 126, 138, 151.

The Author

Sue Heady was born in Botswana and lived there for three years until her parents moved to Seychelles. She enjoyed an idyllic childhood on the islands during the 1970s, before her family moved again, this time to Hong Kong where she lived until 1993. She has always maintained a great affection for Seychelles and has returned to her former home on numerous occasions in recent years. A freelance journalist and author, she is now based in England but continues to travel frequently.

Index